Museum of East Asian Art

Berlin

Prestel
Munich · London · New York

Front cover: Zhang Lu (ca.1490–ca. 1563),
Playing the Zither for a Friend (see p. 50)
Back cover: The Japanese Tea Room in
the Museum of East Asian Art
(Photo: Iris Papadopoulos)

Texts based on contributions by:
Elisabeth von Campenhausen,
Herbert Butz (HB), Antje Papist-Matsuo,
Uta Rahman-Steinert (RS), Khanh Trinh
(KT), Willibald Veit (WV)

Translated from the German by
Elizabeth Schwaiger, Toronto
Japanese poems translated by Yasuko
Betchaku and Joan B. Mirviss
Edited by Margaret E. Taylor, Toronto

Editorial direction: Christopher Wynne

Prestel Verlag
Mandlstrasse 26, 80802 Munich
Tel.: +49 (89) 38 17 09-0
Fax: +49 (89) 38 17 09-35;
4 Bloomsbury Place, London WC1A 2QA
Tel.: +44 (020) 7323-5004
Fax: +44 (020) 7636-8004;
175 Fifth Avenue, New York, NY 10010
Tel.: +1 (212) 995-2720
Fax: +1 (212) 995-2733
www.prestel.com

Die Deutsche Bibliothek CIP-Einheits-aufnahme data is available

Design: Maja Kluy, Berlin
Lithography: LVD, Berlin
Printing and binding: Passavia
Druckservice GmbH, Passau

Printed in Germany on acid-free paper
ISBN 3-7913-2460-8 (English edition)
ISBN 3-7913-2458-6 (German edition)

Museum für Ostasiatische Kunst
Staatliche Museen zu Berlin –
Preußischer Kulturbesitz
Lansstrasse 8
Administration: Takustrasse 40
14195 Berlin
Tel: +49 (30) 8301-382
Fax: +49 (30) 8301-501
e-mail: oak@smb.spk-berlin.de

Opening Hours
Tuesday to Friday: 10am–6pm
Saturday and Sunday: 11am–6pm
Closed on Mondays

Cafeteria

Public Transport
Underground: (U1) to Dahlem-Dorf
Buses: X 11, X 83, 110, 183

Recorded Information
Tel: +49 (30) 2090 5555 (24 hours)
For further information:
Tel.: +49 (30) 8301-438
Visit our web site
www.smb.spk-berlin.de

For Information on Guided Tours
Tel.: +49 (30) 2090 5566
Fax: +49 (30) 2090 5501

Digital Gallery
Four computer work stations
in the entrance foyer to the
Museum of East Asian Art

Friends and Supporters of the Museum
Deutsche Gesellschaft für
Ostasiatische Kunst
www.dgok.de
For further information please contact
the Museum

Contents

The Museum of East Asian Art

The East Asian Art Collection, the second museum of non-European art in Germany, was established on November 8, 1906, by ministerial decree as part of the Royal Prussian Museums. Wilhelm von Bode (1845–1929), the general director, was the driving force behind the establishment of the Collection. Two years earlier he had founded the Museum of Islamic Art. In 1913, yet another museum devoted to non-European art was built: the Museum of East Asian Art in Cologne. The newest museum exhibiting non-European art in Germany is the Museum of Indian Art, which was created in 1963 from the collections of the Museum of Ethnology in Berlin.

Wilhelm von Bode's goal was to balance the art museums devoted to European collections with comparable institutions devoted to cultures outside of Europe. No doubt this process was encouraged by the expansionist policies of the Prussian empire (the German colony of Tsingtao in China was established in 1898) and Japan's entry into world politics. As well, world's fairs introduced Europeans and Americans to the cultural achievements of the Far East, and may have influenced European museums to open their doors to cultures beyond the continent.

Otto Kümmel (1874–1952) was appointed as the first director, and he shaped and directed the Collection until 1945. The Freiburg collector and docent Ernst Große (1862–1927) must be acknowledged as the spiritual founder of the museum. Together with Marie Meyer, the widow of a Hamburg industrialist, he compiled the most valuable private collection of East Asian art in Germany with the help of the Paris-based art dealer Hayashi Tadamasa (1853–1906). It was Große's advice and urgency that ultimately convinced Wilhelm von Bode to found the museum. Following his appointment, Otto Kümmel was sent to East Asia to develop the collection together with Ernst Große, who was attached to the German embassies in Tokyo and Beijing as scientific advisor from 1907 to 1913. As early as March 1907 Große and Kümmel were able to make the first significant acquisitions for the Berlin museum from the Hayashi Collection in Tokyo. The acquisitions focused on Japanese painting and tea ceramics, then still fairly unknown in the West, as well as Korean ceramics used for the tea ceremony in Japan and lacquerware. Major works of Chinese painting were purchased in Japan as well as in China. Kümmel's criterion in his acquisition policy was artistic quality; he was not aiming at providing a comprehensive overview of the art of East Asia.

Two generous donations augmented the collection in those early days. The first was the bequest of the Marie Meyer and Ernst Große Collection in 1915, which more than doubled the holdings and significantly raised its overall quality. It centred on Chinese bronzes and Japanese as well as Chinese painting. In 1919 the museum became the beneficiary of the collection of Gustav Jacoby (1857–1921), former imperial Japanese consul in Berlin. It comprised some two thousand objects, including hundreds of exquisite pieces of lacquerware as well as numerous sword fittings. Among the collection was one of the museum's greatest treasures, thirty-six *shikishi* album leaves (see p. 108) with calligraphy by Hon'ami Kōetsu (1558–1637) and painting by Tawaraya Sōtatsu (active c. 1600–1630).

In 1924 the museum established its first permanent galleries in the basement of the Museum of Applied Arts (the present-day Martin Gropius Building) in the Prinz-Albrecht-Strasse (modern Niederkirchnerstrasse). The facilities were noted for their "East Asian" proportions and design: suspended ceilings and bright, open rooms. But the museum would remain in its new home for

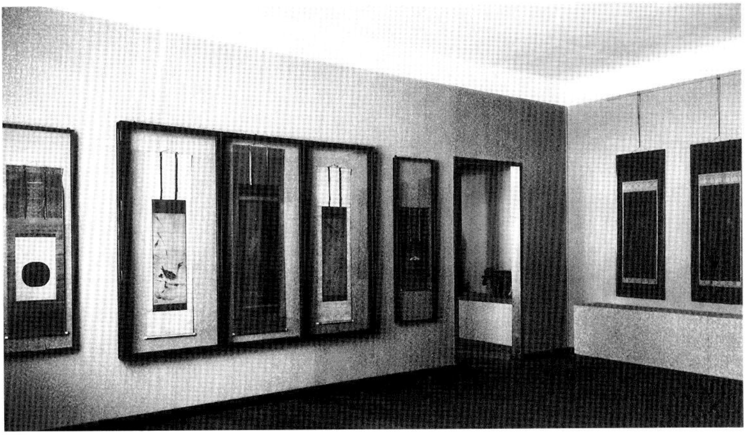

Interior of the East Asian Art Collection, 1924

no longer than some fifteen years. One final acquisition tour took Otto Kümmel to China in 1926–1927. He concentrated mainly on Chinese painting from the Ming and Qing dynasties.

Public relations through special exhibits were especially important for the development of the museum. As early as 1908, Kümmel exhibited the new acquisitions in the Museum of Applied Arts and in 1912, participated in a major exhibition entitled "Ancient East Asian Art" at the Royal Academy of Art in Berlin. The following major exhibitions were mounted in collaboration with the Prussian Academy of Art and the East Asian Art Society: in 1929, "Exhibition of Chinese Art" with 1,250 objects from European and American collections; in 1931, "Works by Living Japanese Painters," eleven artists donated paintings to the museum; in 1932, "China and Japan in the Art Cabinet of the Electors of Brandenburg"; in 1934, "Contemporary Chinese Painting," sixteen works by fourteen artists were presented by the Republic of China as a gift to the Collection; in 1939, "Exhibition of Classical Japanese Art," an exhibition of hitherto unsurpassed art historic significance, funded by the government of Japan.

Leopold Reidemeister (1900–1987), museum curator and, after the war, the first director general of the State Museums of Berlin, Prussian Heritage Foundation, played a significant role in these exhibitions. He was solely responsible for the success of the "Art Cabinet" exhibition, and it is due to his initiative that numerous undated objects in the Ethnological Museum were properly identified.

World War II brought terrible loss and disruption to the Museum. The Martin Gropius Building was destroyed and with it, nearly five percent of the collection was lost. The entire library, including the slide and photograph archives, fell victim to the flames. Ninety percent of the collection had been stored in a bunker near Berlin's zoo during the war and was confiscated by the trophy commission of the Soviet Army as "war booty" at the end of the war just prior to the arrival of the Allies. More than any other museum, the Museum of East Asian Art suffered from this action on the part of the Soviets. Most of the collection remains in the Hermitage Museum in St. Petersburg. Some 300 objects, predominantly Chinese and Japanese paintings, selected pieces of Chinese applied arts, and many pieces of Korean and Japanese tea ceramics had been moved to safety in the mines near Magdeburg in Saxony-Anhalt as late as 1945. After the war they were returned to West Berlin and became the core stock from which the Museum of East Asian Art was rebuilt in Dahlem. When the returned treasures of the collection were exhibited for the first time in 1963 in the 'Haus am Waldsee', Leopold Reidemeister wrote in the foreword to the catalogue: "It is not without sadness that we will revisit these works from the East Asian Art department of the State Museums of Berlin. There is sadness because in seeing them once again we feel only too keenly what we have lost, what we must now forever relinquish. And it is hardest of all for the one who was allowed to collaborate for nearly two decades with Otto Kümmel and William Cohn in building the collection, only to see all these efforts destroyed. The war and its consequences have hit this collection harder than all other museums in Berlin ..."

In other words, it was difficult to imagine a new beginning for the museum after the war. The high quality of the pieces that had been safely returned to West Berlin, however, encouraged deliberations on how to rebuild the collection. In the end, it is thanks to Leopold Reidemeister as director general that the Museum of East Asian Art was reinstated. To ensure the success of this endeavour, Reidemeister appointed Roger Goepper as museum director in 1959. During his time in office until 1966 several important acquisitions were made, including the Chinese ceremonial axe (see p. 11), one of the best-known objects in the museum today. Under the leadership of Beatrix von Ragué, director from 1966 to 1985, the collection was systematically expanded by important single acquisitions and also entire collections. Painting and lacquerware, and also archaic bronzes, were particular areas of focus. The transfer of the woodblock print collection from the Art Library to the museum in 1967 was a milestone for the Collection. In 1970, twenty-five years after the destruction of the museum, a new permanent home was once again established for the East Asian Art Collection in Dahlem. And in 1988 the acquisition of the Jungfische Collection allowed the Museum to regain its former renown in the area of Chinese painting.

Many Jewish collectors and patrons had built the original collection, and this tradition was once again in evidence when Lotti and Gerd Wallenstein, who had fled Berlin in 1939, donated their collection to the Museum through the Cosmopolitan Arts Foundation in New York. It consisted mainly of Chinese woodblock prints but also applied arts.

In East Berlin, the East Asian Collection was set up soon after the war in the north wing of the Pergamon Museum. This collection comprised East Asian pieces from the Museum of Applied Arts and East Asian export ceramics, mostly dating from the 17th and 18th centuries, from Monbijou Palace, which had been destroyed in the war. In 1959 the collection in East Berlin was greatly augmented through a gift from the People's Republic of China of 251 objects ranging in date from the Neolithic period to late imperial period. The gift was presented on the occasion of the tenth anniversary of the foundation of the German Democratic Republic. The highlights of this generous gift are the porcelains and lacquerware from the Ming and Qing dynasties, formerly housed in the Palace Museum in Beijing. Another valuable addition to the collection was the donation of the Franz Carl Weiskopf (1900–1955) and Grete Weiskopf (Alex Wedding, 1905–1966) Collection. The good relationship with the People's Republic of China and the lively exchange of scientists and technicians up to the period of the Cultural Revolution made it possible to build an extensive collection of contemporary Chinese painting, the second main focus of the East Asian Collection.

Since January 1, 1992, the former West and East Berlin collections have been housed together in Dahlem under the name Museum of East Asian Art. The East Asian Collection from East Berlin had a strong ethnological cast; thus, on reunifying the two collections, nearly three-quarters of the approximately five thousand pieces were transferred to the East Asian section in the Museum of Ethnology in Dahlem. In 1996 the museum acquired the Klingenberg Collection with support from the Ernst von Siemens Foundation of Munich, an acquisition that went some way towards compensating for the painful loss of the original Chinese bronze collection.

The reunification of the State Museums also led to the amalgamation of the two museums of Islamic Art. The Dahlem institution returned to Museum Island, which enabled the Museum of East Asian Art to double its exhibition space and to develop a new exhibition concept. Klaus Friedrich Naumann, a Berliner now living in Tokyo, made a generous offer that came at a fortuitous time for the museum and moved the development plans forward: Naumann's private collection of East Asian Art, consisting mainly of lacquerware and Japanese painting, would be available to the museum as a loan for a period of ten years. Valuable individual objects from his collection will be donated to the museum, and one of the fourteen permanent galleries in the museum will be devoted to this collection.

Another private collection from Berlin will add an entirely new focus to the museum. The Yuegutang Collection comprises Chinese ceramics from the Neolithic age to the Song dynasty with nearly three hundred objects, representing this sector of Chinese arts in all its breadth. This collection will also be available to the museum as a long-term loan.

Three areas of East Asian art that have not been represented in the collection up until now, or only on a very limited scale, will also be featured in the new museum, thanks to loans from Japan and Hong Kong, among others; these are Korean and Vietnamese ceramics, as well as Chinese furniture from the 16th and 17th centuries. The Yuegutang Collection and the Vietnamese ceramics will be documented in separate publications. Thus, the re-opening of the newly conceived and newly designed exhibition signals the active participation of collectors and other museums on an unprecedented scale. This approach to collaboration, especially among museums, will play an ever-increasing role in future permanent exhibitions.

WILLIBALD VEIT
Berlin, September 2000

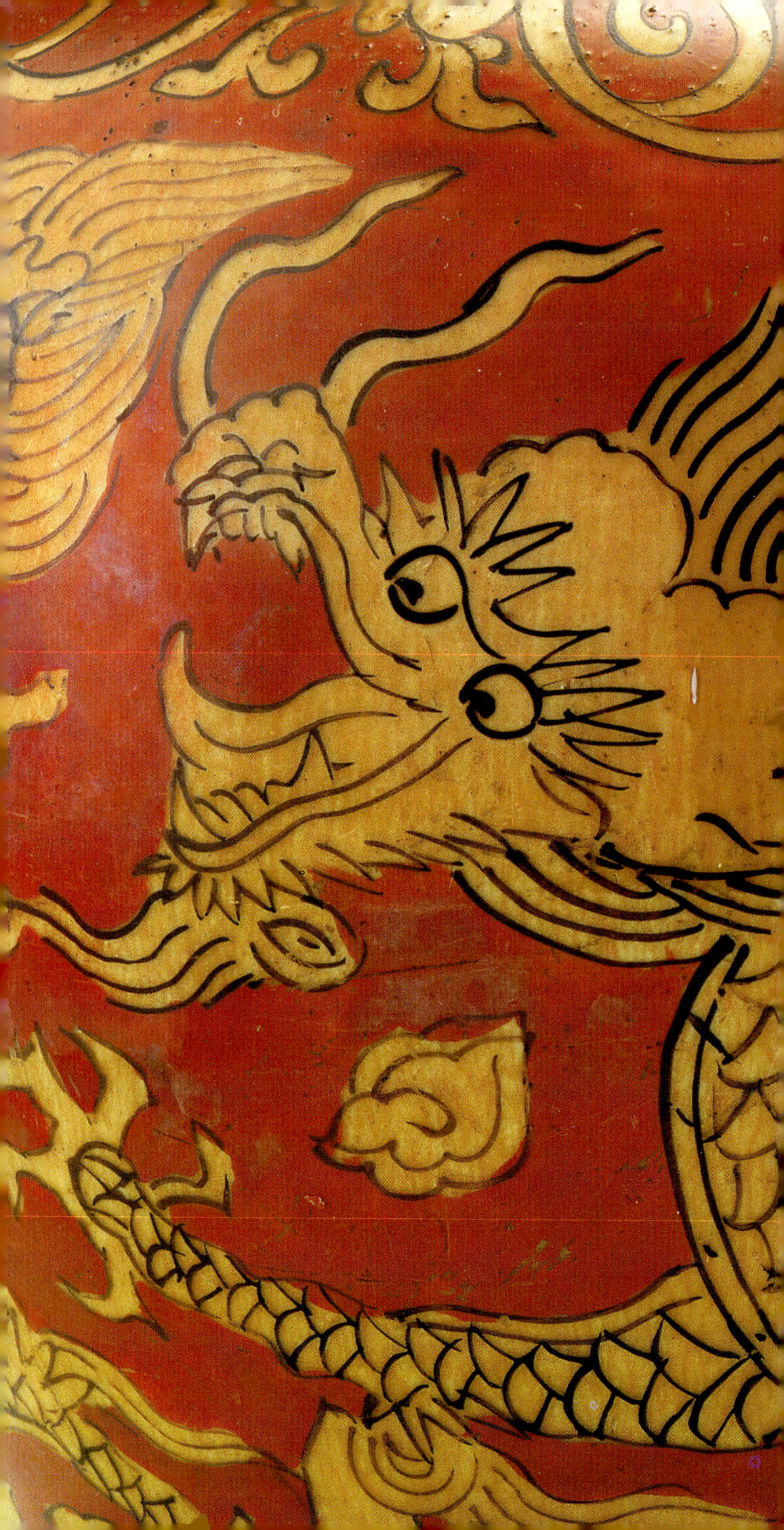

CHINA

Early Chinese bronzes, with which this guidebook opens, have always been a focus in Chinese art collections, and the inscriptions on these bronzes have been especially valued by historians of early China. Early Chinese bronzes have been a special interest of the Museum since its foundation in 1906. The first piece in the collection (Inv. No. 1) was a bronze belt buckle with gold and turquoise inlay from the 5th–4th century BC, a gift from a Berlin art dealer. Under the first director, Otto Kümmel, a widely acclaimed collection was formed within a relatively short period, many pieces of which still remain in the Hermitage Museum (see p. 5). The post-war acquisition policy focused on exquisite individual pieces, such as the famous ceremonial axe (*yue* type) from 12th–11th century BC (p. 11) and the ritual vessel ("Zhaowang *gui*") circa 500 BC (p. 13), as well as acquisitions of specialized collections such as the bronze mirrors from the Oeder Collection and the so-called Ordos bronzes from the Bidder Collection (p. 16). With the acquisition of the Wilhelm and Christine Klingenberg Collection (pp. 12, 14, 15) in 1996 – a marvellous addition to the post-war collection – it was once again possible to offer a comprehensive presentation of the high artistic standard of early Chinese bronzes.

Chinese ceramics, especially of the later periods, were extremely popular among Berlin collectors in the pre-war era, in keeping with well-established European traditions of collecting. It is only in recent decades, however, that the early history of Chinese ceramics has been more comprehensively represented in collections, thanks to new archaeological discoveries. An amphora (*ping* type) from the 5th millennium BC (p. 18) is the oldest exhibit in the Berlin collection. It is one of several important acquisitions of early Chinese ceramics made over the past decades. The pilgrim flask from circa 600 (p. 24), whose ornamentation shows a strong influence from Sassanian Persia, is considered one of the greatest treasures of the ceramics collection. The 11th-century incense burner from the Yaozhou kilns in Shaanxi province (p. 29) is one of the highlights of the collection of northern celadon ware.

The opening of the newly designed museum makes it possible to present the many-faceted development of Chinese ceramics from the Neolithic period through to the Song dynasty in a new and comprehensive manner. This is mainly thanks to the exhibit of an extensive private Berlin collection, known as the Yuegutang Collection, which has been entrusted to the museum as a loan. One of the donations by the People's Republic of China in 1959 to the former German Democratic Republic (see p. 6) was the impressive blue-and-white plate with grape and tendril decoration (p. 31) from the Yongle era (1403 to 1424) of the Ming dynasty. It is a prime example of the splendour and beauty of the collection of Chinese porcelain from the last two dynasties, which has been augmented through generous donations. The exquisite small porcelain stem-cup from the early 17th century (p. 32) has a special historic significance, having been acquired for the Art Cabinet during the first months of the reign of the Elector Frederic III and documented in the inventory compiled in 1688 to 1713.

Chinese lacquerware was also represented among the treasures in the Elector's Art Cabinet. East Asia's great tradition of lacquerware was a focus during the creation of the pre-war collection. Since the new beginning after the war, several important new acquisitions have been made, among them masterpieces of the highest quality. One such masterpiece is the exquisite low table with red carved lacquer (p. 34) from the imperial workshops of the Yongle era. This exhibit as well as the famous imperial throne ensemble (p. 35) – a major work in mother-of-pearl inlay from the late 17th century – came to the museum from the Fritz Low-Beer Collection.

Chinese Buddhist art was represented by major sculptures in the pre-war collection, such as the marble torso of a Bodhisattva from the 6th century (Inv. No. 5110), purchased on the Japanese art market in 1928. One of the most important works in the post-war collection is the figure of the Buddha Amitâbha on a lotus throne acquired in 1960 (p. 38), whose inscription dates the piece to 746. The eleven-headed Bodhisattva Guanyin (p. 39) from the second half of the 8th century, is a masterpiece of bronze art. The important cast-iron sculpture of a "demon" (p. 40), only recently identified as Wuzhiqi, Divine Spirit of the Huai and Guo rivers, was acquired in 1984. For the re-opening of the museum, the collection of Chinese Buddhist art is augmented by three outstanding sculptures (7th–13th century) from the famous collection of Eduard von der Heydt (1882–1964), which are on loan to the Museum from the Rietberg Museum in Zurich.

With the transfer of the East Asian print collection from the Berlin Art Library to the Museum of East Asian Art in 1967, two of the most renowned works of Chinese woodblock prints joined the museum collection. These are the 128 illustrations from the *Treatise on the Paintings and Writings of the Ten Bamboo Studio* (p. 42) from 1633 and four volumes of the *Mustard Seed Garden Painting Manual* (p. 42), published between 1679 and 1701. The collection of Chinese woodblock prints has grown in the past decades through the acquisition of important single works, among them treasured prints from the renowned printing and publishing house of the Ding family in Suzhou, Jiangsu province (p. 43), as well as the donation of the extensive collection of 'New Year Prints' from the Wallenstein collection.

In the hierarchy of the arts in China, calligraphy and painting rank the highest, and the Museum has acknowledged this status in its acquisition policy. The collection is one of the best in Europe. It features Chinese painting from the last seven centuries, from circa 1300 to the present. The selection begins with a fan painting from the 12th–13th century with a landscape featuring water buffaloes (p. 45). The most recent example illustrated in the guide is an album leaf with a landscape by Huang Binhong (p. 65) from 1954. In addition to the genre of landscape painting represented by a series of masterpieces, among them works by leading literati artists, the genre of bird and flower painting is also represented by outstanding works. Among figure paintings, there is the album leaf by Zhang Lu (p. 50 and front cover) from the first half of the 16th century, acquired in 1992, which depicts two seated scholars, one of whom is playing the zither. This work represents the Zhe school, which included the court and professional painters of the Ming dynasty, and which is the counterpart to the Wu school of literati painters. In addition to the treasures from the famous pre-war collection, the guide includes important post-war acquisitions of many paintings (pp. 52–62, 65–67) as well as calligraphies (p. 58) from the extensive Mochan shanzhuang Collection, which were acquired in 1988. Finally, there are numerous works from the 1920s to 1950s (pp. 65–67), providing a link to the present day.

HB

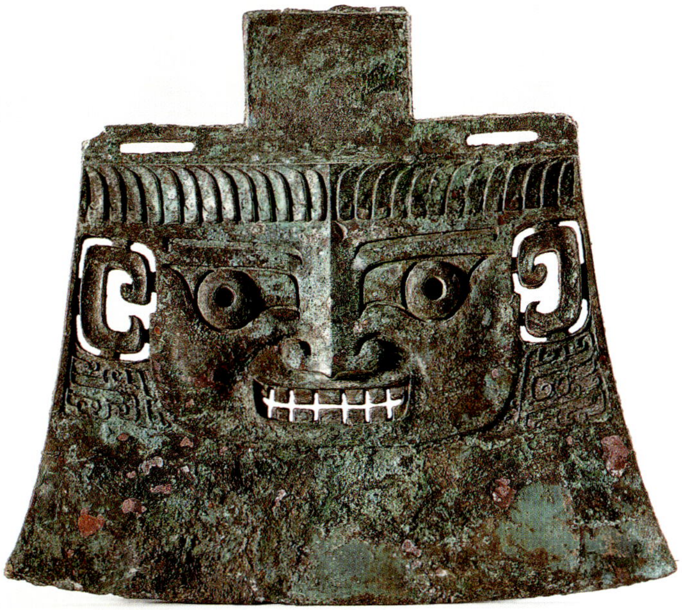

Ceremonial axe, *yue* type

Reported site Xincun, Junxian prefecture, Hunan province
Shang dynasty, Anyang period, 12th–11th century BC
Bronze
Height 30.4 cm, width 35 cm
Weight 4800 g
Inv. No. 1962-4
Formerly Chen Rentao Collection, Hong Kong

The slightly curved blade of the broadaxe is decorated on both sides with a sculptural human mask characterized by large, staring eyes and an open, "smiling" mouth. The teeth and ears are in openwork. To the right and left of the cheek areas are decorative sections in line-relief that are iconographically related to representations of body elements of demons from the Shang dynasty, such as the *taotie* or dragons, two of the dominant motifs found in early Chinese bronzes. The shoulder widens into a rectangular tenon, which together with two horizontal slits served to fasten the shaft. This broadaxe is exceptional in its masterfully rendered, expressive human mask. The only pieces comparable in formal quality were discovered just after the mid-1960s during an excavation of a Shang tomb near Sufutun, Yidu prefecture, in Shandong province. The two broadaxes found there were probably left behind in the tomb once the burial ritual had been completed, which – as numerous skeletal remains indicate – included the ritual sacrifice of forty-eight humans and six dogs. The ceremonial broadaxe, a masterpiece of early Chinese bronze art, was acquired for the Berlin Collection in 1962.

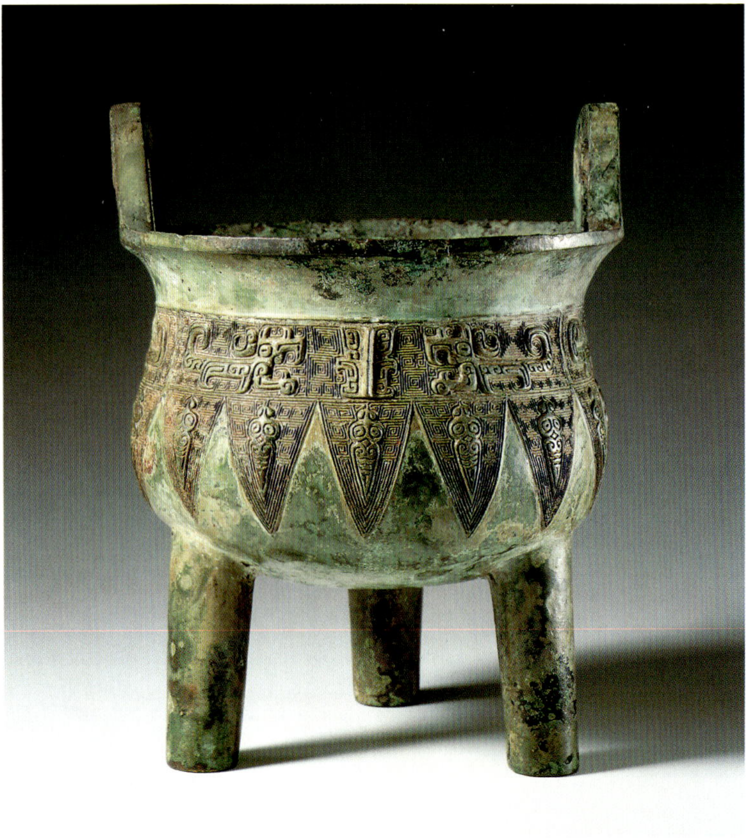

Ritual vessel, *ding* type

Shang dynasty, Anyang period,
13th–11th century BC
Bronze
Height 22.7 cm, diameter (mouth) 18.4 cm, weight 2540 g
Inv. No. 1996-3
Klingenberg Collection
Acquired with the support of the Ernst von Siemens Foundation

Deep, bulbous cauldron with retracted neck on three slightly splayed cylindrical legs. Thick ring handles connect vertically at the lip. The shoulder is wrapped in a decorative band with six bird-dragons, separated at the front and back by a reduced *taotie* mask and a central dividing ridge. On a *leiwen* spiral-patterned ground the bird-dragons are arranged antithetically on either side of the central masks. Striking inverted triangles with a cicada pattern on a *leiwen* background decorate the belly of the vessel.

The powerful proportions of the cauldron, the sturdy legs and thick handles, give the vessel a particularly solid appearance. As one of the dominant types of ritual vessels, the *ding* became a classic in Chinese bronze art.

A pictogram inscribed on the inner wall, just below the mouth of the vessel, shows a kneeling figure holding cowri shells, which were used as a monetary unit in early China. The pictogram indicates the noble family to whom the vessel was originally dedicated.

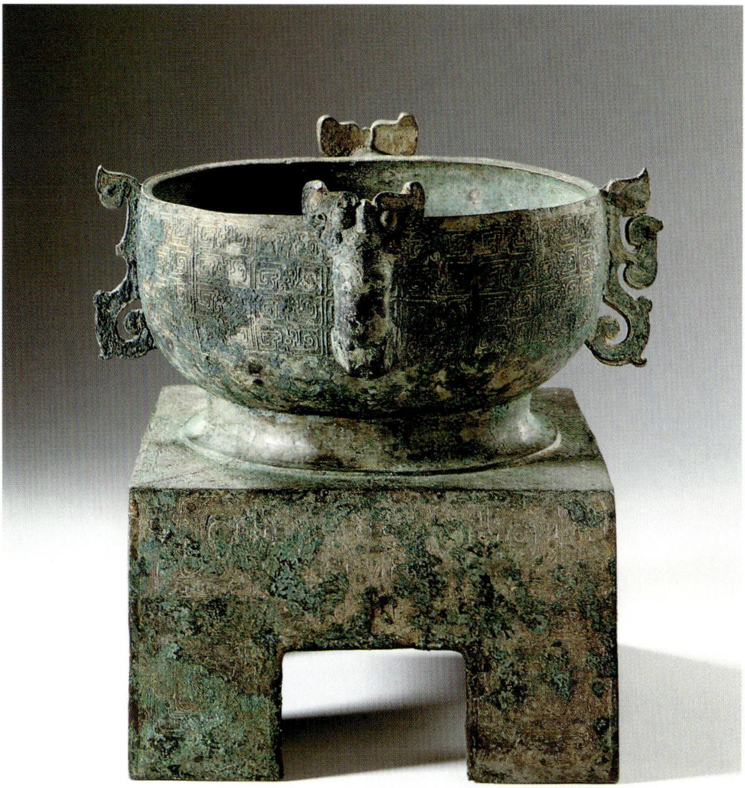

Ritual vessel, *gui* type: Zhaowang *gui*

Shouzhou region, Huai valley, Anhui province
Eastern Zhou dynasty, Chunqiu period, ca. 500 BC
Bronze
Height (without handles) 24.3 cm, height (base) 12.6 cm, diameter 30.9 cm, width (base) 21.3 cm, weight 5325 g
Inv. No. 1970-1

The deep basin of the vessel with a short, extended foot rests on a square pedestal. Sturdy, looped handles with animal heads in relief are set into the sides of the vessel. The walls of the basin are divided into registers with stylized animal designs executed in powerful curving lines. Above the lower handle joint the vessel is decorated with four rows of repeated decorative motifs on a finely hatched background. A stylized animal head is at the centre of each decorative unit. The walls of the pedestal feature entwined ornamental bands with a scattering of eye motifs. A two-column, seven-character inscription on the inside of the basin identifies this *gui* as a ritual vessel of a relative of King Zhao, thus it has become known as "Zhaowang *gui*" (King Zhao's *gui*). King Zhao of Chu's capital was located in Ying near modern Jingzhou on the middle Yangtze in Hubei province. He ruled from 515 to 489 BC. A companion piece is housed in the Shanghai Museum.

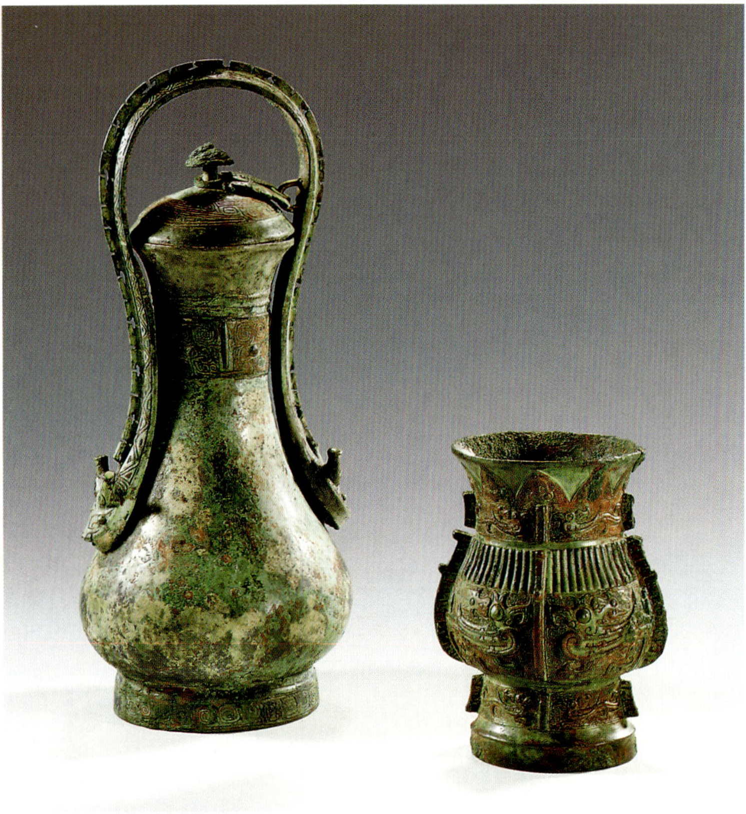

Ritual vessels, *you* type (left, a) and *zhi* type (right, b)

Bronze
a Shang dynasty, early Anyang period, late 13th century BC
Height 29 cm, diameter (mouth) 7.4 cm, weight 1580 g
b Late Shang/early Western Zhou dynasty, 11th century BC
Height 13.2 cm, width (mouth) 8.4 cm, weight 635 g
Inv. No. 1996-11 and 15
Klingenberg Collection
Acquired with the support of the Ernst von Siemens Foundation

a The lidded, pear-shaped vessel rests on a flared foot ring. The movable looped handle terminates in two sculptural horned snake-dragon heads. The lid comes to rest at the handle with a flat connection piece in the shape of a winged cicada. Beneath two bowstrings, the neck is decorated with bodied *taotie*, the whole decorative band being divided into registers with central vertical ridges.
b The bellied beaker stands on a flared foot with a cylindrical base, narrowing towards the neck and opening at the mouth. The main decorative panel, framed at the top by reeding, shows antithetically arranged birds with lush plumage in relief against a fine *leiwen* background. Smaller birds are hidden beneath the abundant tail feathers. The inscription on the inside bottom identifies Wan Fu Ding as the ancestor to whom this vessel was dedicated.

Ritual bells, *niuzhong* type (left, a) and *bozhong* type (right, b)

Reported site Jincun near Luoyang, Henan province
Eastern Zhou dynasty, Zhanguo period, ca. 400 BC
Bronze
a Height (with handle) 28 cm, width (mouth) 16,4 cm, weight 3810 g
Inv. no. 1960-2
b Height 34 cm, width 23.1 cm, weight 11.8 kg
Inv. No. 1996-22
Klingenberg Collection
Acquired with the support of the Ernst von Siemens Foundation

a Ellipsoid in cross-section, the body of the bell widens towards the crescent-shaped mouth. A narrow, tall, undecorated loop, from which the bell was suspended, crowns the covering plate.

On the upper wall of the bell, a nearly square panel is framed on both sides by triple rows of bosses in the shape of coiled snakes. They are arranged around a *taotie* mask in flat relief. The striking panel on the lower wall of the bell features a legless pair of dragons with heads turned in opposite directions arranged on either side of the striking panel.

This bell, like the one from the Klingenberg Collection (b), is an example of the phenomenon of an early form of archaism in Chinese bronzes, with a decorative language that draws on the past.

b Ellipsoid in cross-section, the body of the bell is gently flared from the covering plate to the flat-edged lip. The covering plate is crowned by an openwork loop from which the bell was suspended. It is in the shape of two birds turning their heads back. A large, vertical, nearly rectangular panel framed by pronounced ridges covers approximately one-third of the bell. Within this rectangle, narrow, square compartments are arranged around a plain centre panel. They are filled, alternately, with rows of bosses and horizontal bands with dragon

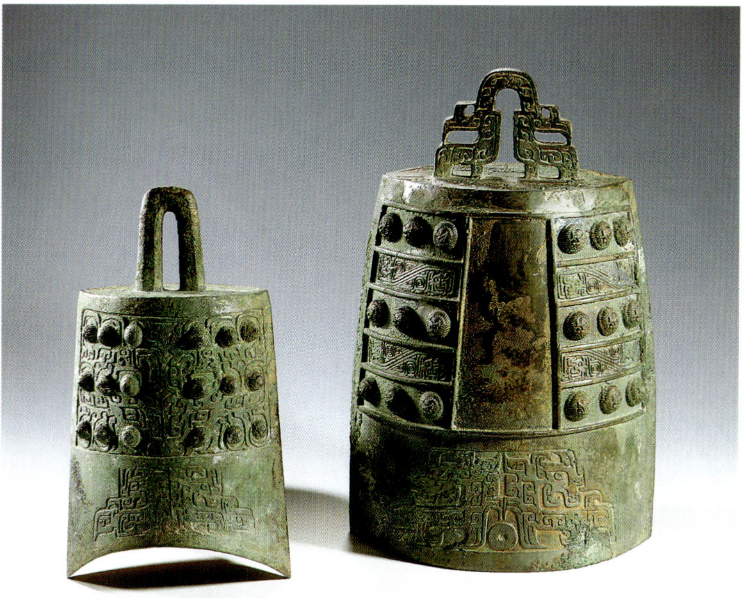

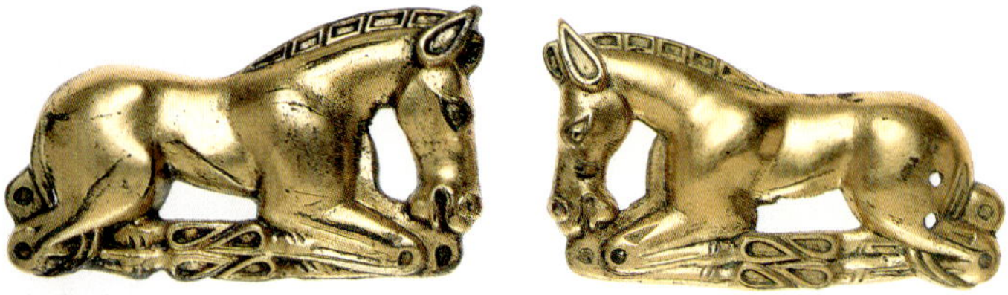

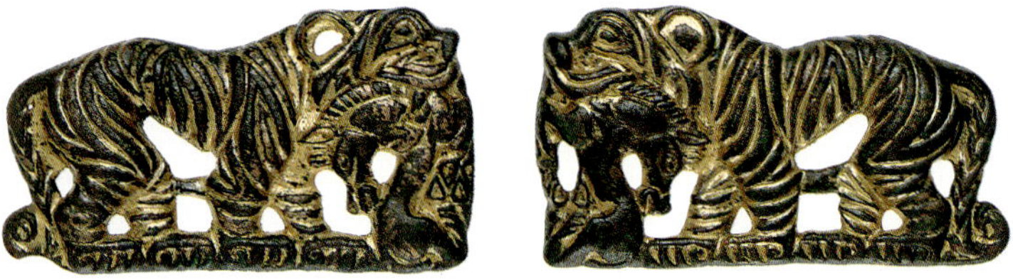

heads. The bosses are in the shape of coiled snakes, topped by snake heads seen from above. The main decorative panel on the lower section of the bell, which is also the surface on which the bell was struck, is decorated with large legless dragons with heads turned back, arranged on either side of the striking panel. The covering plate of the bell also features a pair of facing dragons. These bells were struck in specific sets and sequences during rituals connected with ancestor worship and ceremonial events at court.

Pair of plaques in the shape of (a) reclining wild donkeys and (b) in the shape of tigers and donkey prey

Ordos region in northwest China
Eastern Zhou dynasty, Zhanguo period (480–222 BC)
Gilded bronze
a Height 7.8 cm, width 13.9 cm
b Height 7.9 cm, width 14.7 cm
Inv. No. 1965-23 a/b and 24 a/b
Formerly Dr. Hans Bidder Collection

These beautifully modelled plaques – one pair of reclining wild donkeys and another pair of tigers with donkey prey – count among the "Ordos bronzes." In the first millennium BC, the Ordos region in northwestern China was populated by nomads who belonged to a Central Asian culture that reached far to the west. The Ordos bronzes are predominantly plaques with one or several eyelets on the back, which were stitched onto clothes and horse fittings for decoration. They are almost always decorated with animal motifs, reflecting the mythological beliefs and lifestyle of the nomads for whom these bronze objects were made. In 1965 the Museum was able to purchase a collection of more than a hundred Ordos bronzes, purchased prior to World War II by Dr. Hans Bidder (1897–1952), a diplomat who served in China.

Round mirror

Tang dynasty, 7th–8th century
Bronze
Diameter 22 cm
Inv. No. OAS 1966-9
Formerly F.C. Weiskopf Collection, Berlin

The back of this mirror, richly decorated with motifs taken from flora and fauna and also from mythology, is a type called *ruishou yima putao jing* in Chinese ("mirror with animals, winged horses, and wine grapes as auspicious charms"). Three concentric zones bordered by bosses are arranged around a handle in the shape of a toad-like mythical beast. A narrow band of stylized clouds wraps around the perimeter. Among the multitude of animals and mythical beasts surrounded by vines laden with grapes, two human figures are also visible. The integration of grape and animal motifs, popular during the Tang dynasty, betrays strong influences from Sassanian Persia.

Mirrors, which were cast in bronze from clay moulds, have a long tradition in China. The earliest archaeological findings date back to the Qijia culture on the upper Yangtze around 2000 BC. The Museum has some seventy Chinese bronze mirrors in its collection, ranging from the 6th century BC to the 12th century.

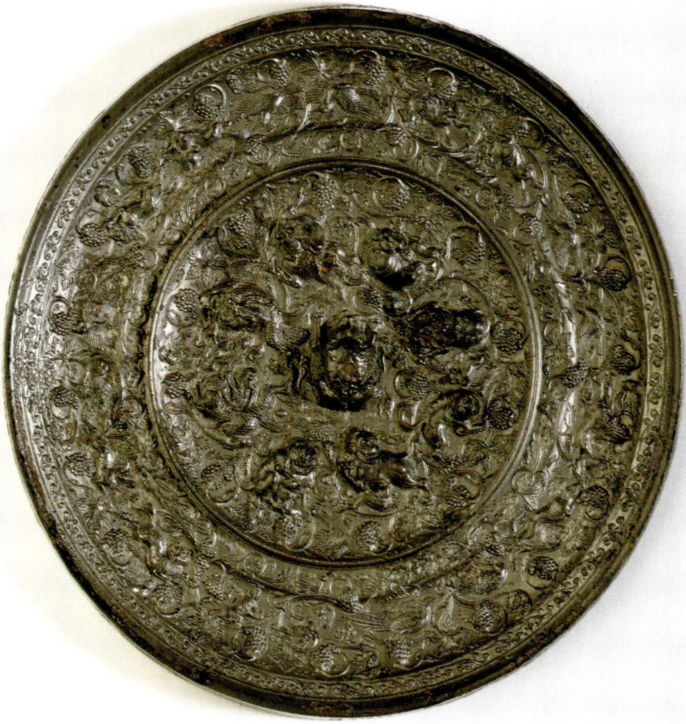

Amphora, *ping* type

Shaanxi province
Neolithic period, Yangshao culture
Banpo type, 5th millennium BC
Red clay with rope impressions
Height 30.4 cm, diameter (mouth) 6.3 cm
Inv. No. 1988-14

The egg-shaped body of the vessel tapering to a point at the bottom has two looped handles, a very narrow neck, and a cup-shaped opening. The upper middle of the body is decorated with a diagonal rope pattern that was created by tapping a rope-covered piece of wood against the clay. In a similar piece consulted for comparison, the plain section above the rope pattern was covered with painted decoration.

In shape this amphora, intended for carrying water, is typical of Neolithic ceramics of the Yangshao culture, which developed along the middle section of the Yellow River (Huanghe) circa 4800 to 3000 BC. The amphora is classified as Banpo ceramic, produced circa 4800 to 4300 BC and named after a Neolithic settlement near Xi'an in Shaanxi province.

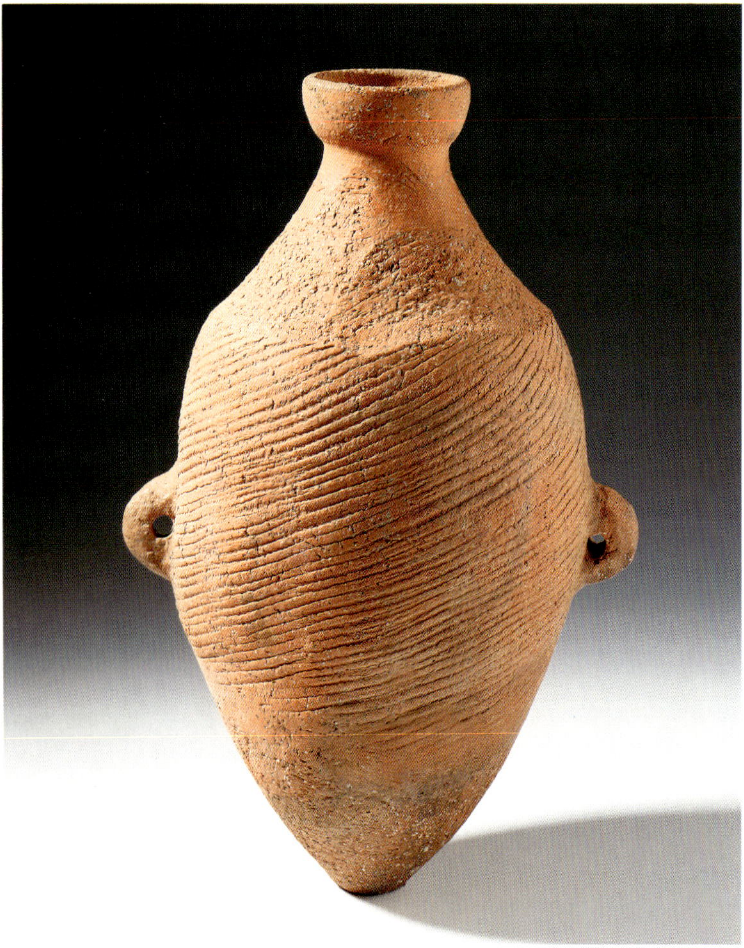

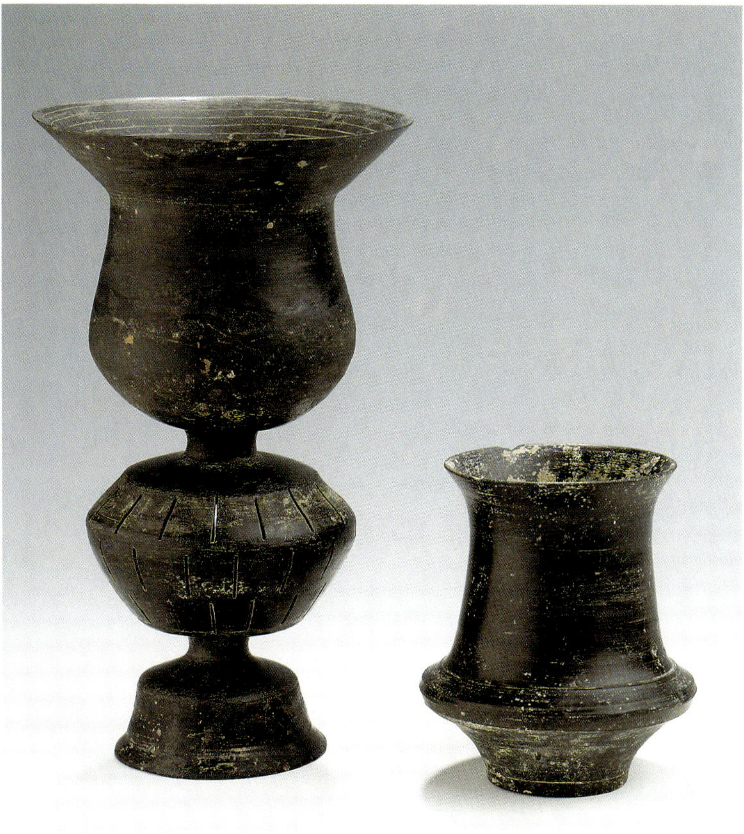

Beaker and hollow-foot beaker

Shandong province
Neolithic, Longshan culture
(ca. 2400–2000 BC)
Black pottery
Height 10.5 cm and 29.7 cm
Inv. No. 1993-7 and 21

Ceramics in fanciful shapes are typical findings of the late Dawenkou culture (ca. 4300–2400 BC) and the Longshan culture (ca. 2400–2000 BC), which succeeded it and spread along the lower section of the Yellow River (Huanghe) in Shandong province. These were made on the potter's wheel and then trimmed to an extraordinary thinness and lightness. In addition, the ware was polished to a high gloss.

This beaker and hollow-foot beaker count among the principal types discovered from this period. The thin-walled beaker in fine black pottery rests on a flat base. It is bulbous in the lower third and opens slightly at the mouth. The equally thin-walled beaker with a wide mouth features a stem with a typical rounded middle section marked by fine, vertical slits. The Longshan potters were extraordinarily inventive in designing such openwork pieces and creating shapes for these types of foot beakers.

Tripod, *Yueshi ding* type

Zhejiang province
Eastern Zhou dynasty, Zhanguo period, 5th–4th century BC
Proto-porcelain, glazed
Height (with loop handles) 17.1 cm
Inv. No. 1988-39

The deep, flat-bottomed bowl with a wide mouth and raised lip rests on three splayed, ribbed legs. Two slightly angled loop handles are attached to the inner side of the raised lip. The stoneware vessel has a yellowish green, irregularly flecked celadon glaze.

Tripods of this kind were discovered together with other types of vessels – all are related to earlier bronzes. They are from tombs in Shaoxing, Zhejiang province, and in Guixi, Jiangxi province, dating from the period of the state of Yue, which was destroyed by Wei Wang, the king of Chu, in 334 BC. Ceramic copies of bells are also among these archaeological finds. These vessels and musical instruments made of stoneware fired at high temperatures – called proto-porcelain because of their outstanding hardness and impermeability – were an economic alternative to the costly bronzes, many of which were buried in tombs or used for offerings to the ancestral spirits.

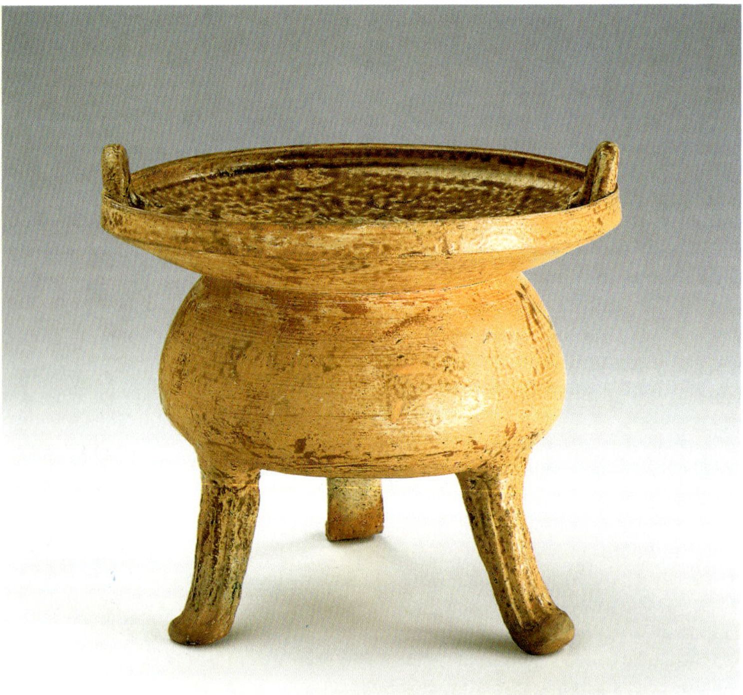

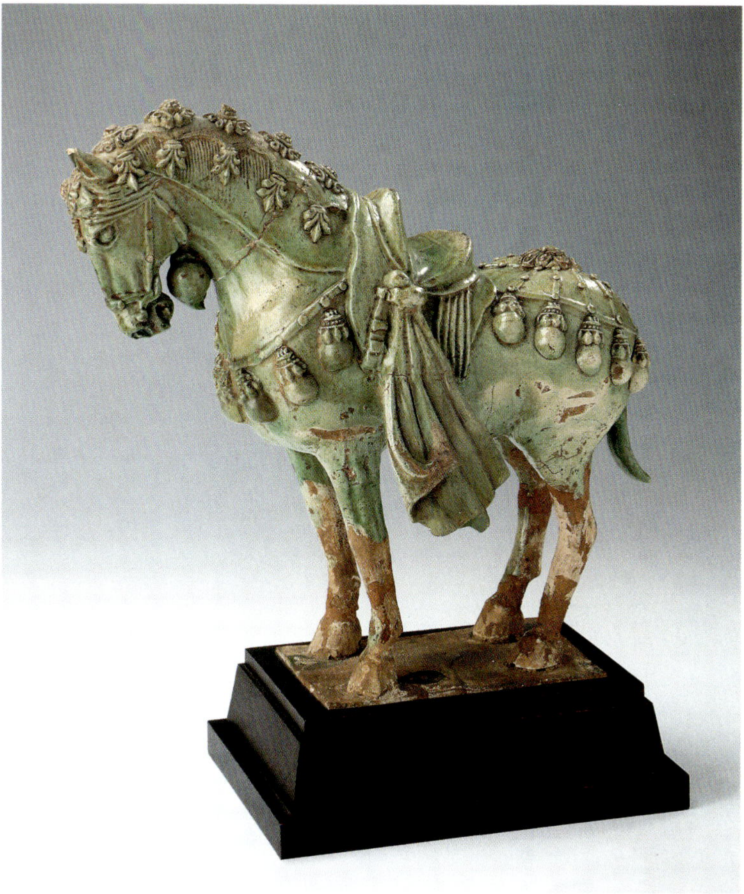

Saddled and bridled horse

Sui dynasty (589–618)
Height 27 cm, l.33 cm
Sand-coloured earthenware with light-green glaze over a white slip
Inv. No. 1958-8
Formerly Fritz Blüthgen Collection, Berlin

The saddled and bridled horse stands erect on a rectangular floor plate with its head turned slightly to the right. It is particularly impressive for its extraordinarily ornate, plastic rendering of the harness ornamentation in the Sassanian style. An unusual feature is the palmette mane ornamentation – a reference to influences from the Middle East that reached China via the ancient trading routes of the Silk Road. Ornamental horse decoration in palmette form has been traced back to the 5th to 4th century BC in Pazyrik (Altai) and later in the Persian region. In China, the horse was a valuable commodity for trading and offering tribute, and equestrian knowledge was highly developed, as is eloquently proven in the tomb art of the time. The horses of Fergana enjoyed particular fame. Equestrian culture peaked in the Tang dynasty (618–906).

Chicken-head ewer

Yue ware, Zhejiang province
Eastern Jin dynasty (317–420)
Earthenware with grey-green glaze and ferruginous spots
Height 21.5 cm, diameter (mouth) 8.1 cm
Inv. No. 1989-17

The bulbous vessel rises from a flat base, with the tall neck ending in a wide funnel opening. The handle joins the lip and the shoulder of the vessel. The short spout is shaped in the form of a fully sculpted chicken-head. Two curved lugs are attached at the shoulder. In its overall contour the form of this vessel is reminiscent of the *hu*-type ewers. The Chinese name for chicken-head ewer (*jitouhu*) seems to confirm this connection. General names for ewers in Chinese such as *bahu* and *zhihu* (both "ewer with handle") point to an alternating play between different formal and typological influences.

Yue ware produced in the north of Zhejiang province – hard-fired earthenware covered in an even glaze – reached its peak during the period of the Six Dynasties (222–589). While ornamentation in the form of applied moulded animal masks and decorative pattern impressions were popular during the Western Jin period (256–316), the vessels of the Eastern Jin period are characterized by sparse ornamentation, exemplified in this ewer with randomly scattered ferruginous dots.

Figure of a lady

Tang dynasty, first half of 8th century
Sand-coloured clay with three-colour (C: *sancai*) glaze
Height 60.3 cm
Inv. No. 1993-33
Donated by Hanna and Walter Brednow, Jena

The tall figure with a three-colour glaze depicts an elegant lady in floor-length dress with a wide shawl around her shoulders and draped over her crossed hands, from which

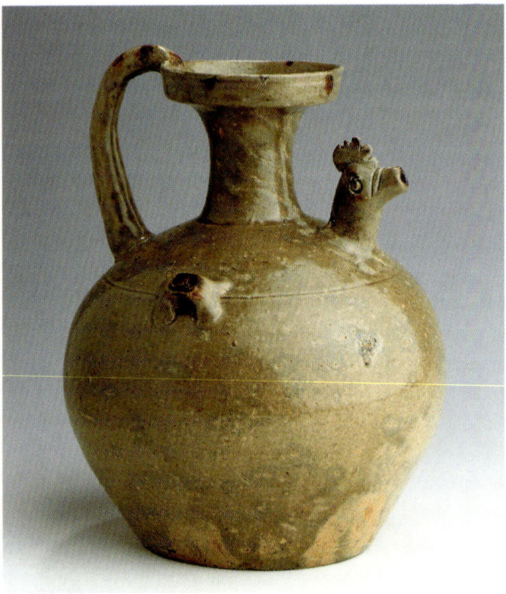

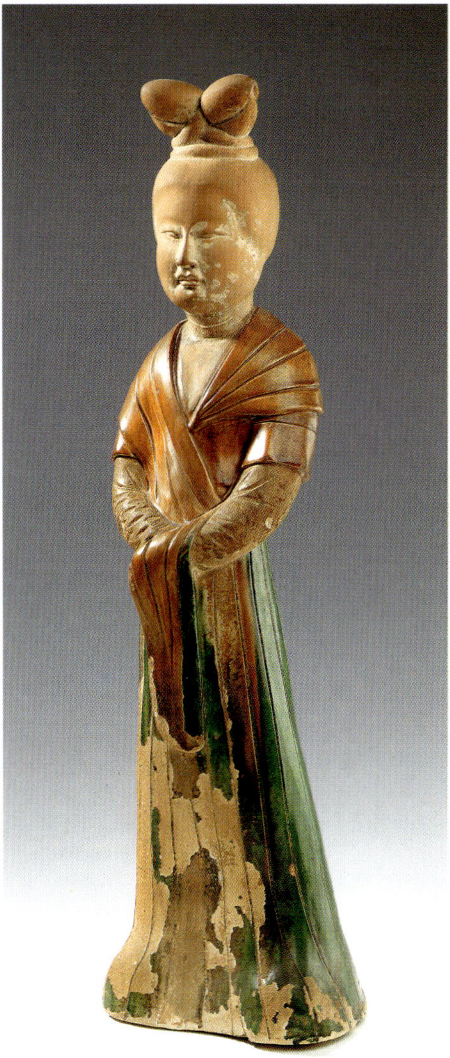

the long ends of the shawl cascade to the ground. The full face, finely modulated nose, and sensual mouth express the ideal beauty of the time. In keeping with the fashion of the period, the coiffure is arranged in a striking double knot. Pottery figures of this kind, which served as tomb offerings, were usually formed from a mould.

Details, such as the pleats indicated by notches, were added by hand. As was typical for figures in multi-coloured glazes, the flesh-toned sections were mostly masked off during glazing and then hand-painted after the figure had been fired. Lead-coloured ceramics called *Tang sancai* experienced a golden age from the late 7th century onwards for approximately a hundred years. Green, amber yellow, and white is a typical combination used in the coloured glazes of this type of pottery.

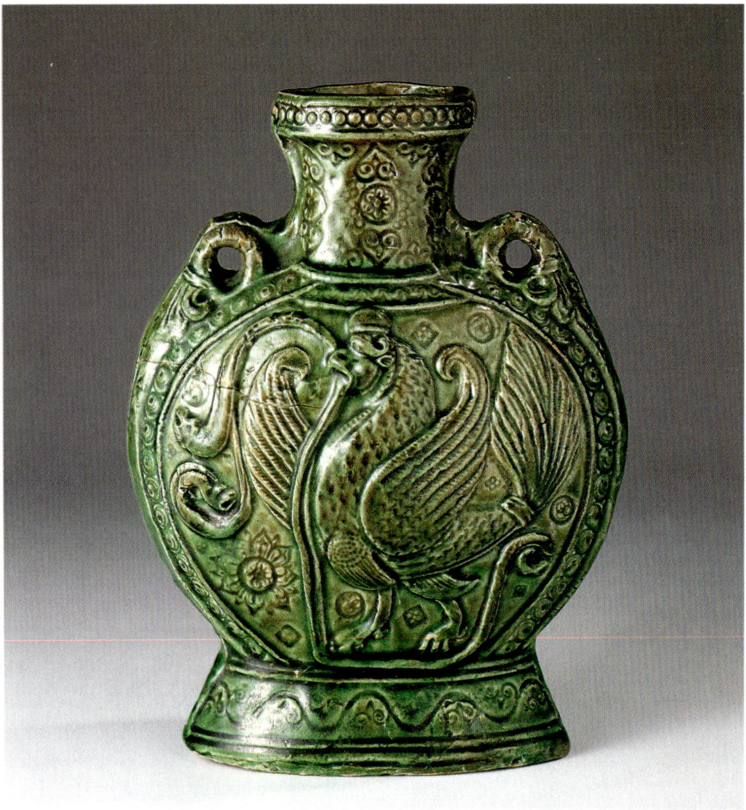

Pilgrim flask, *bianhu* type

Sui or early Tang dynasty, ca. 600
Earthenware with light-coloured body and green glaze
Height 18.5 cm, width 14.7 cm
Inv. No. 1958-6

The flattened pilgrim flask with a wide, flared foot is composed of two identically decorated halves formed in a two-part mould. At the shoulder are two sturdy round lugs which blend into palmettes. The central panel in a frame of "pearls" is dominated by a heraldic bird with a full tail tied with a ribbon and massive wings that coil at the tips. Standing on a vine, the bird's beak holds the end of the same vine bifurcated into two snakes at the tip. The background of this central panel is densely decorated with stylized flowers in different shapes. The pilgrim flask counts among the treasures of the Berlin Collection. Its design is derived from Sassanian Persia transmitted via Central Asia. Such "borrowed" imagery is typical of the appreciation for foreign motifs and shapes which reached its peak in the cosmopolitan China of the Tang period.

Three-footed dish

Tang dynasty, 8th century
Earthenware with reddish body and three-colour (C: *sancai*) glaze
Height 6.3 cm, diameter 29.3 cm
Inv. No. 1986-8

The three-footed dish features an impressed medallion-like decoration in a three-colour glaze of amber yellow, green, and blue. The deepened contours of the ornamental motifs stopped the colours from mixing. A white, slightly yellow slip is painted under the transparent glaze, showing the colours at their most luminous.

An eight-petal flower motif in the centre is surrounded by a matching circle of eight lush lotus blossoms and flowers. The colours of the *sancai* ("three-colour") palette and the strict symmetry of the design, unusual in Chinese pottery, are further testament to the penchant for "exotic" decorative language popular in the Tang dynasty. This piece is described as a *sanzu pan*, a "three-footed plate."

Silver works from Sassanian Persia may have served as models for such designs. A tripod dish from the renowned collection of Michel Calmann at the Musée Guimet, Paris, is decorated with a similar pattern. A flying crane occupies the centre of the eight-tiered lotus flower motif depicted on the dish in Paris.

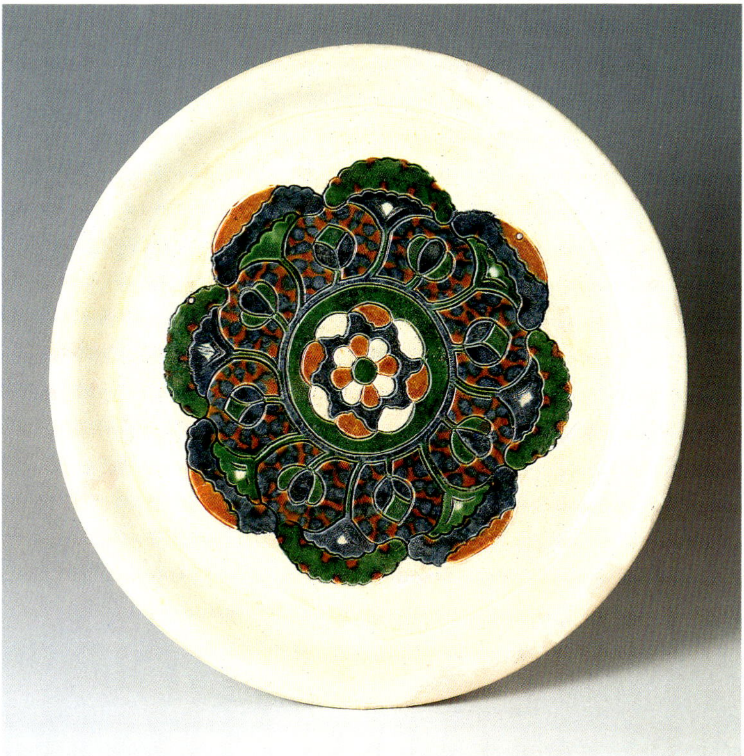

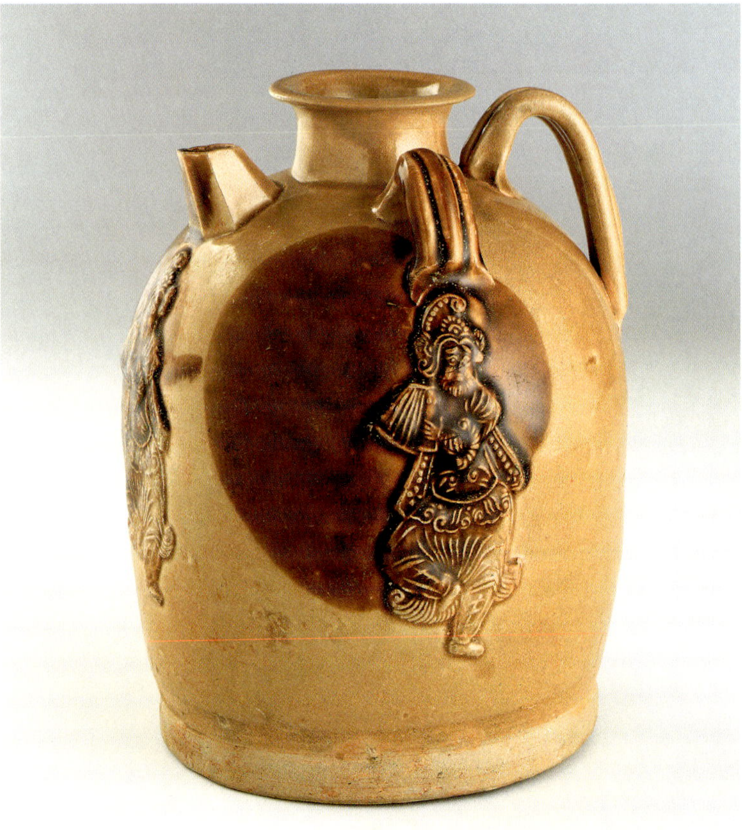

Ewer with applied decoration

Changsha, Hunan province
Tang dynasty, 9th century
Stoneware, glazed, Tongguan ware
Height 18.7 cm
Inv. No. 1988-41

The ewer with a three-strand handle and a short, octagonal spout has a flared, flat-bottomed base. Two lugs – also three-stranded – are attached at the shoulder. Three moulded applied ornaments representing foreign musicians decorate the surface beneath the lugs and the mouth. The appliqués are covered in dark brown glaze marks, typical for this ware.

The ewer originates from the Tongguan kilns near Changsha, Hunan province, where the production of such stonewares with yellow ash glaze and moulded relief motifs flourished and was even exported to Southeast and South Asia. Another popular product of the Tongguan kilns were ewers with painted underglaze decoration.

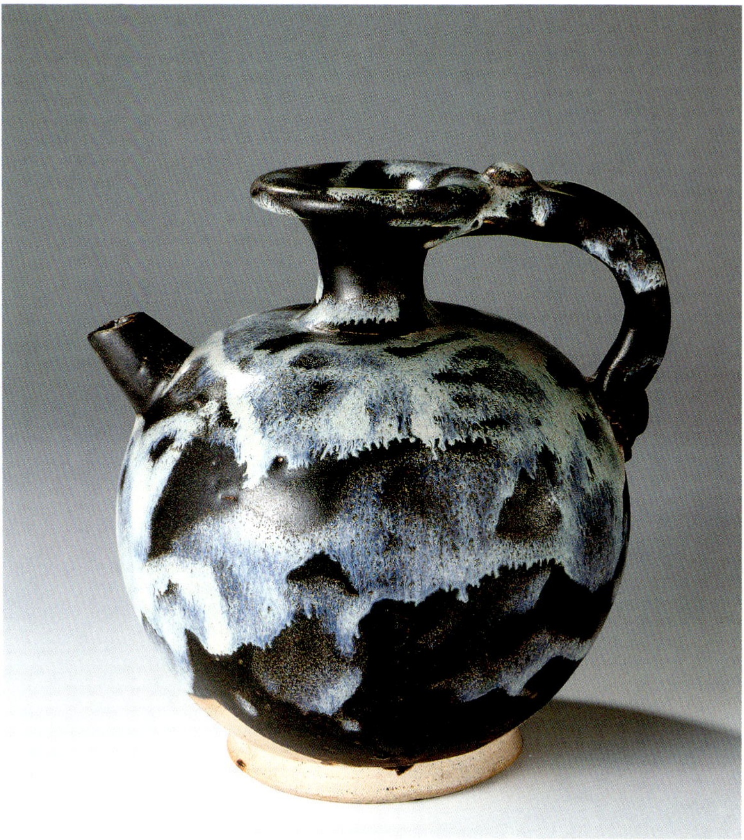

Ewer with *Tang-Jun* glaze

Henan province, Huangdao ware
Tang dynasty, 9th century
Stoneware with light blue spots on black glaze
Height 16.4 cm, diameter 14.5 cm
Inv. No. 1968-17

This masterfully crafted ewer, exceptional for the expressive play of colours in the glaze, has the stout, conical spout typical of this period. The double-stranded handle connects the lip and the shoulder, with "buttons" at each end similar to metal vessels of comparable shape. On a matte black glaze the jug is decorated with blue-white mottling. This is considered a precursor to the Song-dynasty *Jun* ware and is therefore sometimes called *Tang-Jun* or also black *Jun*. The flat-bottomed, flared foot and a few spots on the lower surface are left unglazed.

This black ware with bluish white spots is called Huangdao ware after the kilns at Huangdao in Jiaxian district, Henan province. It has also been traced to other production sites in Henan and Shaanxi, evidence that it was more widely distributed.

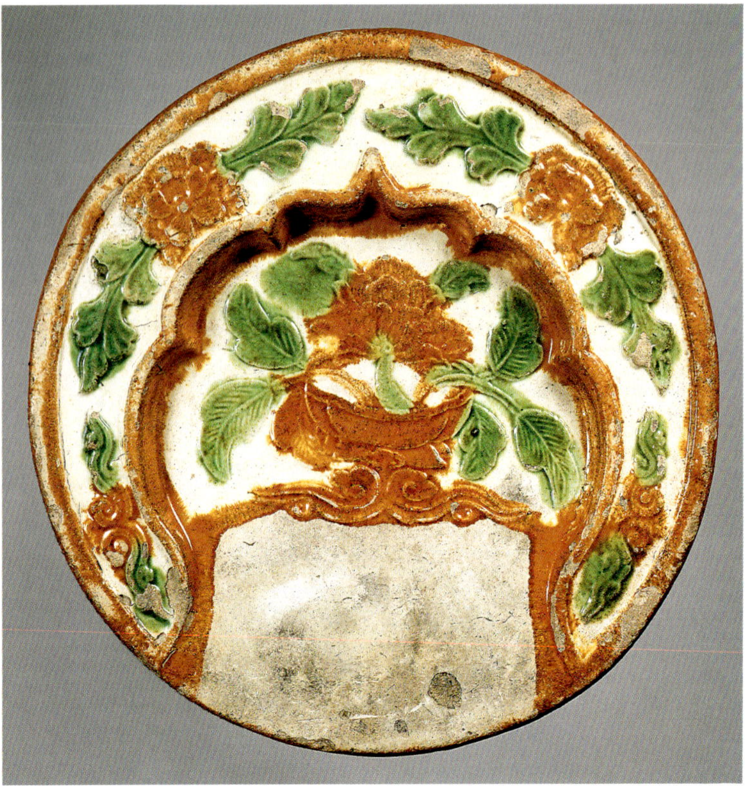

Inkstone

Northern China
Liao dynasty, 11th–12th century
Stoneware with white, amber-yellow, and light-green glaze
Height 6.6 cm, diameter 18.3 cm
Inv. No. 1966-22

The round inkstone shown from the top, features moulded decoration in the shape of peonies and chrysanthemums. The unglazed portion of the slanted, leaf-shaped section is for rubbing the inkstick. While the surrounding top surface of the inkstone is decorated with peonies, the base is ornamented with six lotus-leaf panels with chrysanthemum motifs. The light colour palette of the glaze is typical of Liao ceramics limited to white, amber yellow, and green.

With this glazing palette, the ware is clearly influenced by the three-colour decoration (*sancai*) of the Tang dynasty (618–906). The shapes are often imaginative and even include naturalistic ceramic renditions of stitched leather flasks, examples of which are included in the Berlin Collection. Under the dynastic name of Liao, Tungusic Khitan nomads ruled over wide areas of northern China, Manchuria, as well as Mongolia from the 10th to the 12th century.

Incense burner

Shaanxi province
Northern Song dynasty, 11th century
Stoneware with grey-green celadon glaze, Yaozhou ware
Height 19.4 cm, diameter (mouth) 18.6 cm
Inv. No. 1968-14

Acquired in 1968, this incense burner is one of the treasures of the Berlin Collection – a masterpiece from one of the most glorious periods of Chinese ceramics.

An extraordinary feature of this piece are the five nude figures of foreigners kneeling on the wide base with their backs to the stem. The bowl is decorated with incised patterns. A stylized floral design embellishes the wide, flat lip. The tall fluted wall is decorated with downward-facing pointed leaves with vertical zigzag designs. The production of this type of green glazed stoneware, usually embellished with densely engraved floral motifs, was concentrated in the Yaozhou kilns in the district of Tongchuan, Shaanxi province.

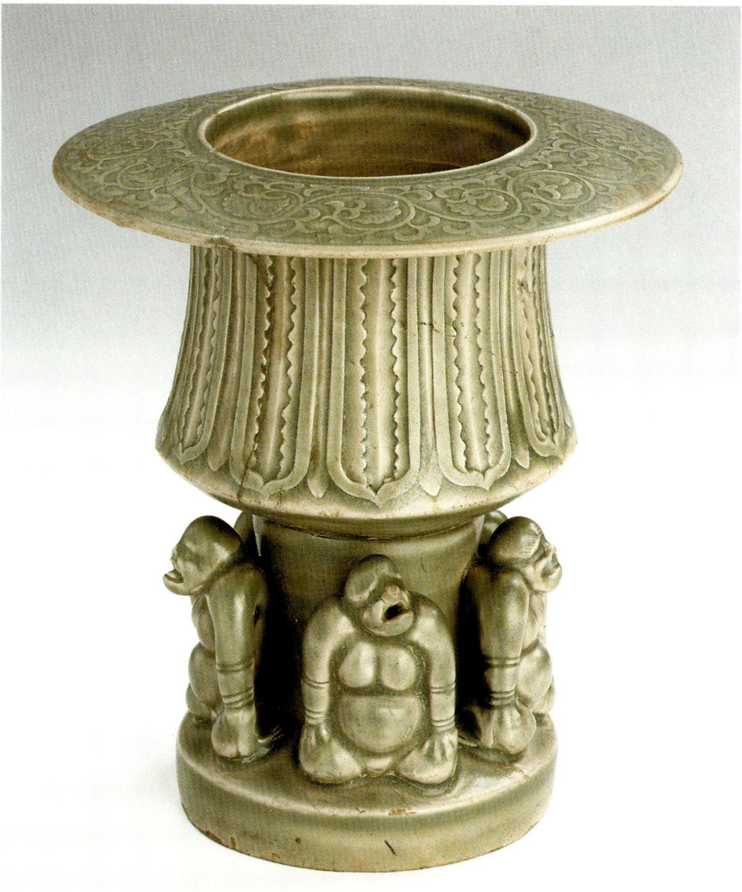

Stoneware headrest with landscape motif

Jin dynasty, 12th–13th century
Stoneware with dark-brown decoration painted over a white slip, Cizhou ware
Height 13 cm, width 26.6 cm
Rectangular impressed cartouche: Zhang jia zao ("Made by the Zhang family")
Inv. No. 1966-30

A landscape genre image, surrounded by a scalloped border, decorates the inclined top surface of this headrest. To the left, a man stands near a group of trees on a spit, gazing at the opposite shore, where a waterfall tumbles from a steep, rocky overhang. The high walls of the headrest are embellished with stylized tendril motifs executed in a generous and spontaneous painterly manner. The white-slip ground provides a strong colour contrast for the dark brown painting.

This everyday ware known for its robust shape and the freshness and immediacy of its decoration was manufactured not only in Cizhou (the Ci district in modern Hebei province), but throughout northern China. The stoneware headrest in the Berlin Collection with its emotive landscape is one of the most beautiful painted examples, especially popular during the Jin dynasty, founded by the Jurchens.

Ceramic pillows, which served as cooling headrests during the summer months, were popular in the Tang dynasty (618–906), and were commonly produced in a number of the most important kilns in the Song and Yuan dynasty (10th–14th century). Not only the headrests of the vernacular Cizhou ware were popular, but also the more elaborate products of the Ding and Yingqing kilns, which captivated through the diversity of their shapes and refinement of their decoration.

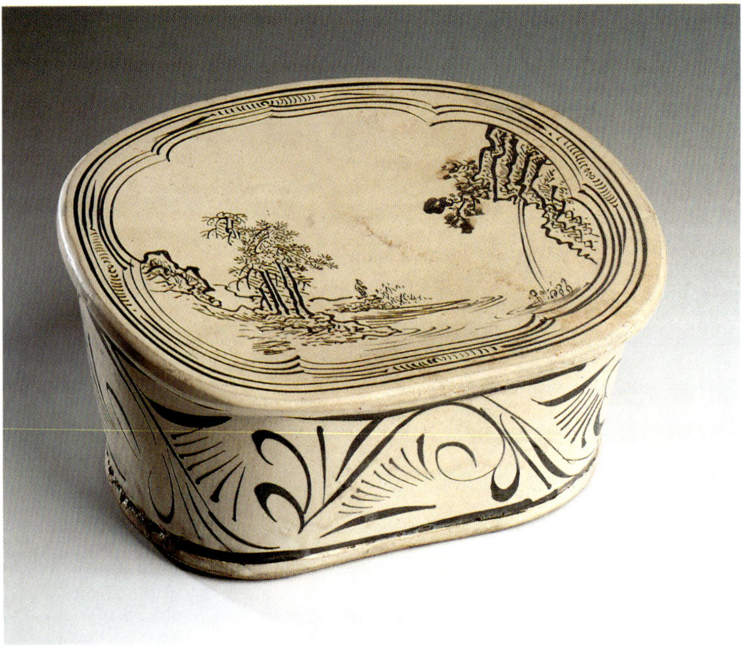

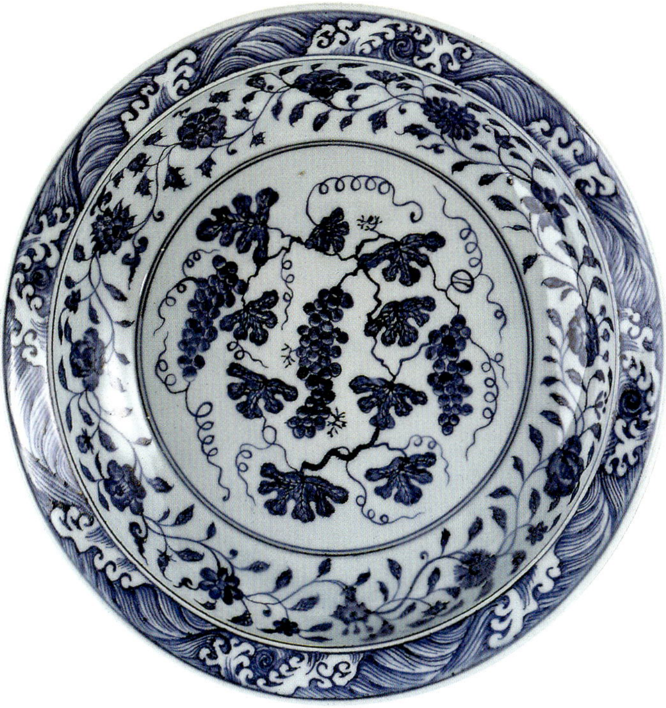

Plate with grape and tendril decoration

Ming dynasty, Yongle era
(1403–1424)
Blue-and-white porcelain
Height 7.2 cm, diameter 37.2 cm
Inv. No. OAS 1959-60
Gift of the People's Republic of China

Porcelain with underglaze-blue decoration conquered the world soon after it was first produced during Mongolian rule in China, the Yuan dynasty (1271–1368). Following the height of blue-and-white porcelain in the second half of the 14th century, the city of Jingdezhen in Jiangxi province gradually became the most important centre in Chinese ceramic production. The main components in Chinese porcelain are kaolin clay with relatively low iron content and the feldspathic petuntse. The transparent and colourless glaze also consists of petuntse with lime and potash added; this glaze covered the translucent white porcelain and gave it its characteristic lustre. Blue-and-white porcelain owes its intense colouring above all to cobalt oxide which at first was imported from Persia. The thick application of cobalt oxide often resulted in the appearance of dark spots after firing, an effect created by the oversaturation and bleeding through of the pigment, which gave the blue-and-white porcelain of that era its unique character. This elaborate plate from the early Ming dynasty also has this unique charm. The centre is decorated with grapes and vines surrounded by a floral band, while waves and ocean spray ornament the rim.

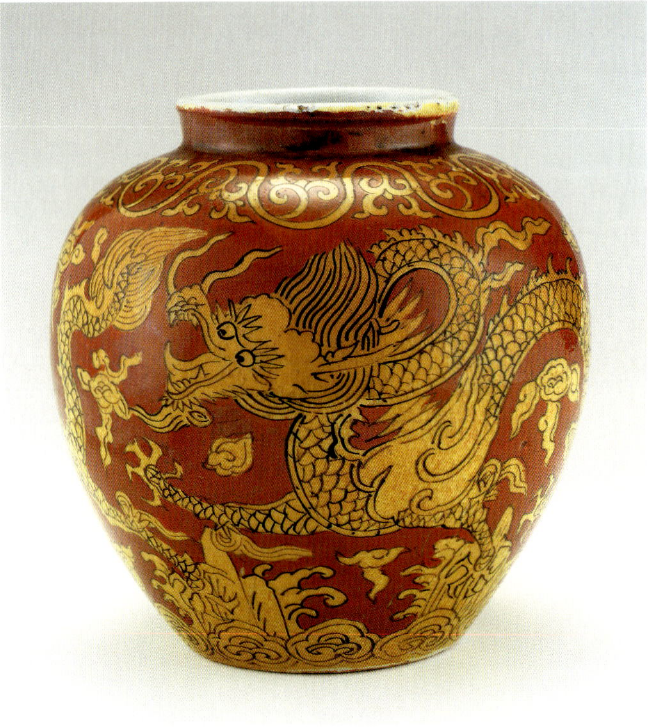

Jar with dragon motif

Ming dynasty, Jiajing era (1522–1566)
Porcelain with yellow and red glaze and brown interior drawing
Height 21 cm, diameter. 21.4 cm
Underglaze-blue mark: *Da Ming Jiajing nian zhi* ("made in the Jiajing era of the Great Ming Dynasty")
Inv. No. 6274
Formerly in the Collection of the Albrecht branch of the Royal House of Prussia

Above rocks against which waves are breaking, two five-clawed dragons are shown chasing each other among the clouds. The bands of clouds are decorated with the auspicious charms called *ruyi* ("whatever you wish"). A stylized, meandering vine embellishes the shoulder, while the base is decorated with an impressive, continuous cloud-scroll border.

The dragon is one of the principal motifs in Chinese art. Since time immemorial it has been regarded in China as a harbinger of important and auspicious events. The five-clawed dragon was widely understood as a symbol of imperial power and authority.

Small stem-cup with openwork panels

Late Ming dynasty, "Transitional Period," first quarter 17th century
Underglaze-blue porcelain, enamels and gold
Height 7.5 cm, diameter (mouth) 6.5 cm
Underglaze-blue mark: *Da Ming Wanli nian zhi* ("made in the Wanli era of the Great Ming dynasty")
Inv. No. 6532.
Formerly Collection of the Elector of Brandenburg

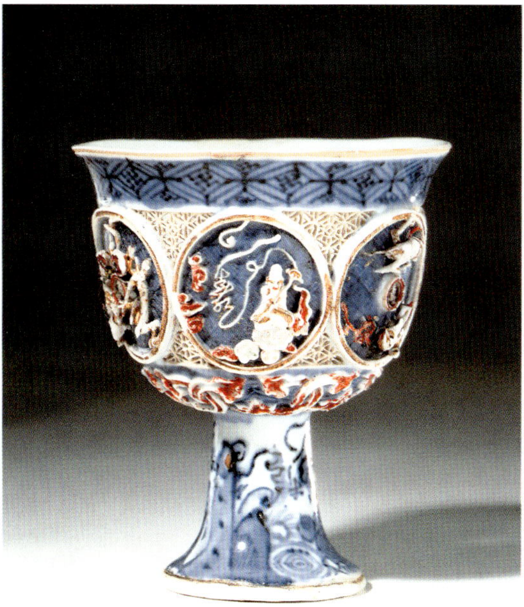

The tall, flaring foot of the small stem-cup is decorated with images of waves breaking against rocks. The bowl of the cup sits upon the foot like the Daoist "Island of the Immortals." The main decorative zone of the cup has six medallions with fine line-relief of images paired with auspicious characters, all set against an openwork background with a star pattern. The central medallion visible in the illustration shows the God of Long Life next to the character *shou* ("long life") in relief set between clouds. The characters in the other medallions are done in openwork. When read in sequence they express: "Ten thousand times good luck, ten thousand times wealth, ten thousand times long life." The reliefs depict bats, stags, dragons, cicada, etc., demonstrating the common practice in the popular pictorial language of using characters with double meanings. Thus the image of bats (pronounced *fu* in Chinese) in one of the medallions is a reference to the character for luck (also pronounced *fu*).

Wang Gongqi
Two tea bowls in the shape of peach halves

Yixing, Jiangsu province
Qing dynasty, 18th century
Ochre and reddish stoneware
Height 5 cm, diameter 8.2 cm (left); height 4 cm, diameter 7.8 cm (right)
Inv. No. KGM 79.1492 and 79.1493
Acquired by Max von Brandt

The handles of the two tea bowls in the shape of peach halves are formed by branches whose foliage and flow-

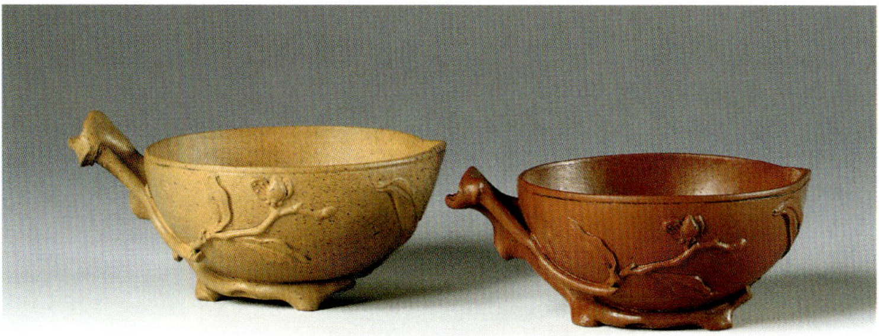

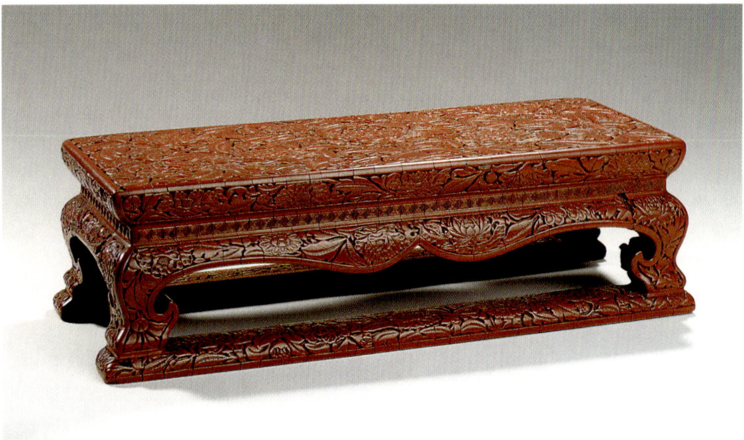

ers spread along the sides of the bowls. On the ochre-coloured cup to the left, the area around the spout is attractively accentuated with a splash of reddish brown. The mark of the potter Wang Gongqi appears just below where the handle joins the side of the cup. Stoneware from Yixing was known in Europe as early as the 17th century. It arrived in Europe together with shipments of the highly valued China tea, was much appreciated and soon copied (e.g., Böttger stoneware). The two tea bowls are among the pieces acquired by the German diplomat Max von Brandt (1835–1920), who was the imperial envoy to Peking from 1875 to 1893 and contributed greatly towards establishing German collections of East Asian art and culture.

Low table

Ming dynasty, Yongle era
(1403–1424)
Carved red lacquer on yellow ground
Height 14.9 cm, width 20.7 cm,
length 52.8 cm
Inv. No. 1978-3.
Formerly Fritz Low-Beer Collection,
New York

This low table with floral decoration is a masterpiece of Chinese carved lacquerwork from the early Ming dynasty. Based on the evidence of two closely related pieces in the collection of the Beijing Palace Museum, it is clear that this piece is also a product of the imperial workshops. Two famous masters renowned for their lacquerwork, Zhang Cheng and Yang Mao, were active during the early Ming dynasty, laying the foundations for a great flowering of this art, which reached its peak in the Yongle (1403–1424) and Xuande periods (1426–1435). The carved lacquerwork on this low table is impressive for the soft handling of the carving into the thick lacquer layers and the compositional elegance of the whole. The table top is decorated with half or fully opened peony blossoms and buds in varying sizes. The table legs and horizontal braces, equally decorated with peonies, are also embellished with blossoming plums, lotus, and chrysanthemum flowers.

Fritz Low-Beer (1906–1976), from whose collection this work was acquired, began to collect Chinese lacquerware as early as 1920 and was able to gather an extensive collection within a few years. Following an exhibition in Amsterdam in 1938, he successfully managed to transfer his entire collection to safety in the United

States when he emigrated. During and after World War II, Low-Beer continued to improve the collection. Today, the bulk of the collection is housed in the Linden Museum in Stuttgart, which acquired the pieces (186 lacquerworks) in 1978. Individual important works of lacquer art had previously been acquired by the Museum of Fine Arts, Boston, the Victoria and Albert Museum, and the British Museum, London. In 1972 the Berlin Collection succeeded in acquiring the famous throne ensemble described below; in 1978 the low table shown in this figure was purchased from the estate.

Imperial throne

Qing dynasty, third quarter of 17th century
Rosewood with inlay in mother-of-pearl, gold and silver foil, coloured lacquer and gold paint
Height 105 cm, width 106 cm, length 73.5 cm
Inv. No. 1972-15. Formerly Fritz Low-Beer Collection, New York

Among the preserved pieces from the imperial workshops, the throne and triptych screen with mother-of-pearl inlay (not pictured) represent a major achievement of the early Kangxi era (1662–1722). The elaborate scenes depicted on image panels with a gold ground on the sides of the throne achieve an impressive play of colours by means of countless mother-of-pearl pieces with a pink, purple and green iridescence. This effect is enhanced by the borders on the frames, which reveal a high level of technical mastery and artistic design.

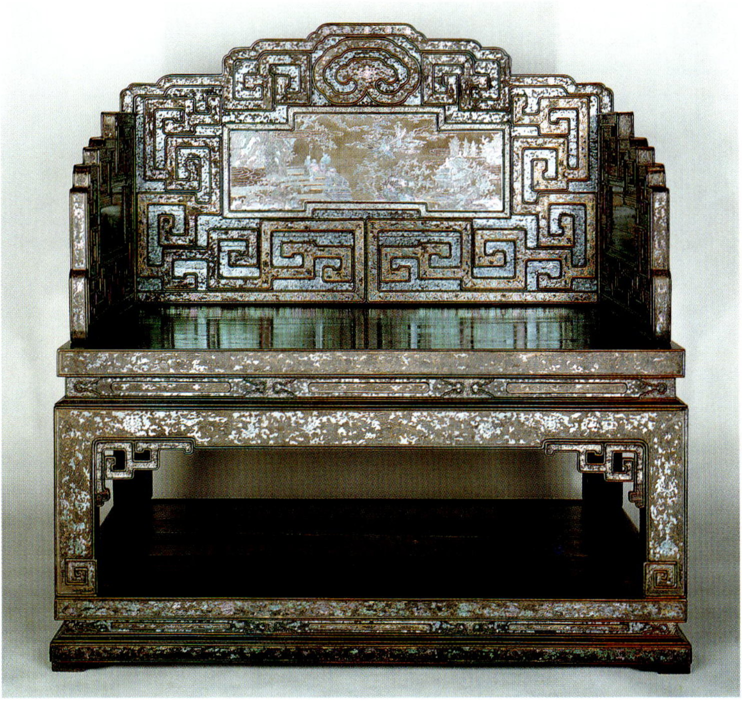

The extravagant ornamentation in this ensemble bears messages with good wishes for a long life and auspicious sayings of all kinds. The main theme in the image panels on the inner sides of the arm and back rests of the throne, as well as in the three large image panels on the outward-facing side of the screen, is the Daoist paradise, which was ruled by Xiwangmu, the Queen Mother of the West. The depictions on the throne show excerpts of the mountain and lake landscapes with terraces, pavilions and palaces which are shown in all their majestic scale on the screen. Xiwangmu is represented as she glides down on a phoenix to alight in this paradise, where her arrival is eagerly awaited by the immortals. In the images on the throne and on the screen, the "eight Daoist immortals" are shown in a prominent position. On the central panel of the screen they are gathered on the large, middle terrace, while countless other immortals populate the paradisiacal landscape on land and in water. On each inner side of the armrests, four of the "eight Daoist immortals" are seen stepping towards the middle terrace, where the deity is expected to alight.

Throne and screen were acquired in 1924 by a French merchant from the previous Chinese owners in Tianjin. As a Chinese document from the time of the purchase indicates, the ensemble originates from the imperial summer palace at Panshan, in the district of Jizhou, Zhili province (modern Hebei province), which the Manchu emperors used on their journey to their summer residence in Chengde, some 250 kilometres northeast of Beijing. China experienced an era of flowering and expansion under the emperors Kangxi (r. 1662–1722), Yongzheng (r. 1723–1735), and Qianlong (r. 1736–1795), during which time it reached the greatest territorial expansion in its history. The grandeur and uniqueness of these emperors is also reflected in the fine arts. Countless variations of imperial representations can still today be seen on many images of emperors on the throne in glorious imperial dress, on occasions of imperial ceremonials, as poets and connoisseurs, as hunters and even as religious figures. The theme on the throne and the screen casts a special light on the ruler's authority based on the heavenly mandate of the emperor, emphasizing the desire that this mandate may last forever. When the emperor sat on the throne, he was, at the centre of the paradise of the immortals, thereby becoming one of them.

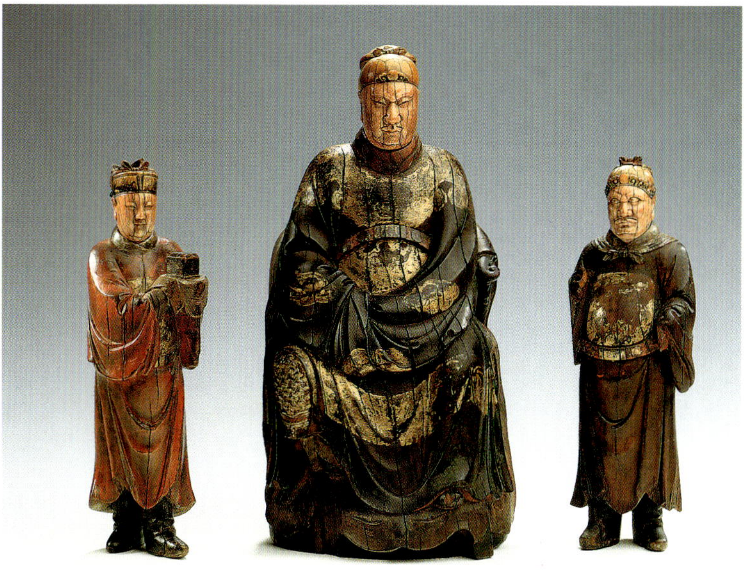

Group of three figures with Guan Yu, the God of War

Ming dynasty, 15th century
Wood and Ivory, extensive traces of the original pigments
Height (a) 29 cm, (b) 23 cm, (c) 22.9 cm
Inv. No. 1991-8 a–c

The group with three figures depicts general Guan Yu (d. 220) in the middle, accompanied by his son Guan Ping to the left and a halberd-bearer, Zhou Cang, to the right. Guan Yu, who was posthumously elevated to the status of God of War, is shown in general's regalia seated on a tigerskin draped over an armchair. His arms are crossed beneath the ample folds of his clothing. The left, bent leg is exposed. The softly modulated face bears grooves for a moustache, sideburns, and chin beard – now lost. The cloak was originally bordered in green and decorated with elaborate painted ornamentation on gold panels. The youthful son wearing a civil servant's hat and red robe carries a square inverted box in his raised hands, which probably contained Guan Yu's official seal. The halberd-bearer – the halberd itself is not preserved – is dressed in a robe that was originally bordered in blue with painting on the gold chest panel. The animal emblem painted in this panel is almost completely rubbed off. Zhou Cang is depicted with a grim mien. Again, the notches and grooves on his face served to attach a beard.

General Guan Yu is a central figure in one of China's most famous novels, *The Romance of the Three Kingdoms* (C: *Sanguozhi yanyi*). He is also one of the most popular figures in Chinese theatre.

Depictions of the general elevated to the God of War and his companions are extremely popular in a wide variety of art forms.

Buddha Amitâbha on a lotus throne

Tang dynasty, 746
Grey limestone with traces of original pigments
Height 94 cm, width (base) 49.5 cm
Inv. No. 1960-4

Buddha Amitabha is seated in the lotus position on a lotus throne with a rectangular base. His left hand rests on the left knee, the missing right hand was probably positioned in the *abhaya* mudra, a gesture meaning "fear not." Only fragments remain of the *mandorla* body halo.

The front and sides of the base bear a donor inscription, with additional names of donors wrapping

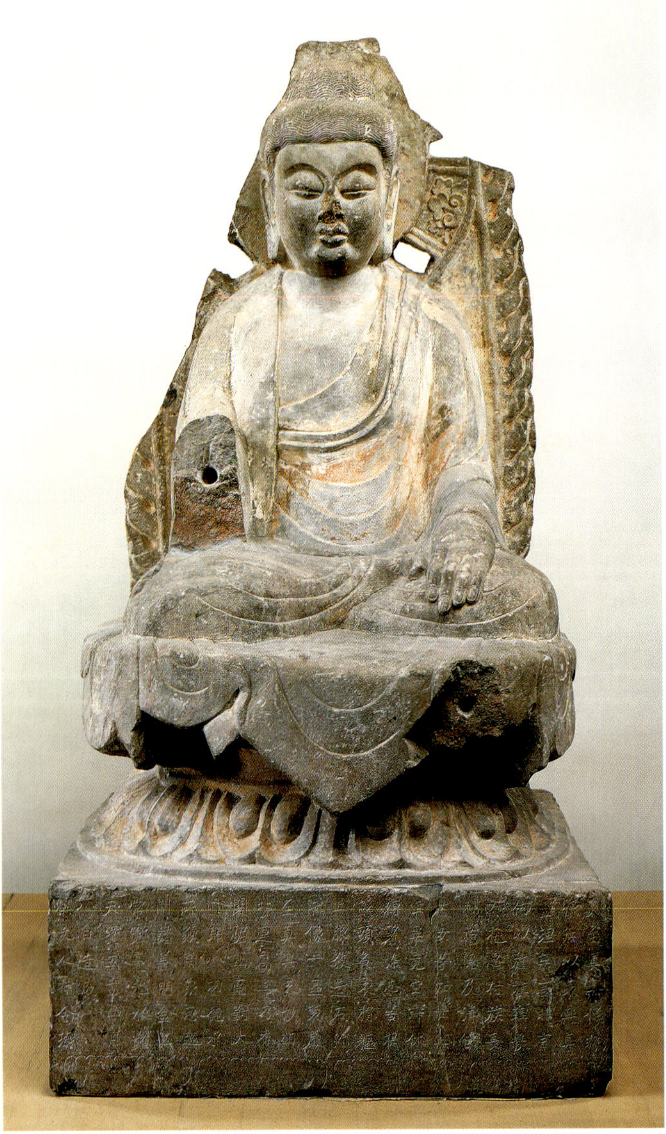

around the back. The inscription identifies a clan elder by the name of Du Fuyin from the village of Baozhong and his family, who are said to have commissioned this figure of a stone Mituo (Amitâbha) despite great personal hardship. The inscription also contains the date of completion: the 8th day of the 4th month of the 5th year of the Tianbao era (746). The Buddha Amitâbha (Buddha of Infinite Light) is one of the great salvation figures in the Buddhist pantheon. Presiding over the Western Paradise, he is the central figure in the Pure Land (C: *Jingtu*) tradition of Mahayana Buddhism, which took hold in China in the 4th to 5th century and soon attained widespread popularity.

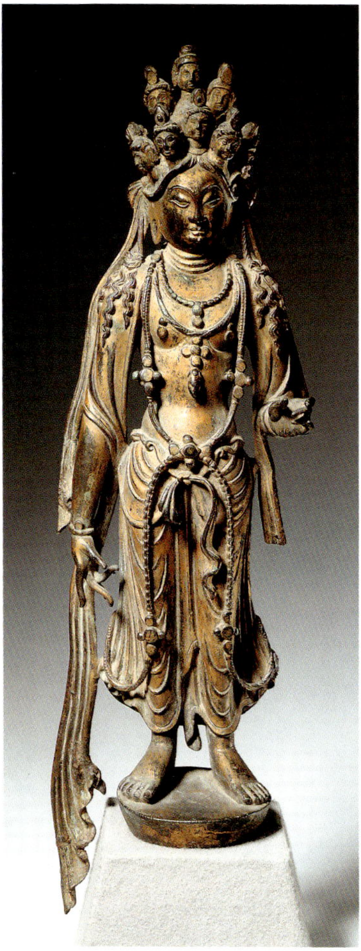

Eleven-headed Bodhisattva Guanyin

Tang dynasty, second half of 8th century
Bronze, gilded
Height (with robe sleeves) 40 cm
Inv. No. Dlg. 10-1973

This exquisite small bronze depicts the eleven-headed Guanyin ("The Deity Gazing with Compassion upon Mankind"; C: *Guanshiyin pusa*) with soft, rounded features and feminine lines. The richly decorated Bodhisattva is dressed in a finely draped robe whose sleeves reach to the ground (the drape on the right side has been lost). One legend explains the eleven-headed aspect of this Bodhisattva by telling how compassion for human suffering caused his head to burst into eleven pieces. The Buddha Amitâbha formed eleven heads from these pieces and placed them on the Bodhisattva. They symbolize the principle of salvation in many forms.

Wuzhiqi, Divine Spirit of the Huai and Guo rivers

Song dynasty, early 12th century
Cast iron
Height 39 cm, width 32 cm, depth 38 cm
Inv. No. 1984-510
Estate of Hanna Bekker vom Rath

The horned "demon," his chin propped on his right hand, which rests on his left knee, faces his viewer in a crouched position with an introspective expression. He supports himself with his left hand, while the right leg, stretched forward and slightly bent, rests on the heel. He wears bracelets around his wrists and ankles.

This expressive sculpture was formerly part of the renowned art collection of painter and art patron Hanna Bekker vom Rath (1893–1983), who left it to the Berlin Museum in 1984. Poul Andersen was only recently able to solve the puzzle of the identity of this figure, which was previously catalogued simply as a "demon." Andersen refers to a 1934 study by Huang Zhigang on Chinese Water Spirits, in which a very similar figure is illustrated and interpreted as Wuzhiqi, the figure having been excavated in the northern part of Henan province and bearing an inscription that dates it to the third month of the year 1101.

Wuzhiqi is the simian divine guardian of the rivers Huai and Guo, which cross in Anhui province, where the cult of this spirit has been documented. It also bears some resemblance to the Japanese water spirits (*kappa*). Two other examples, very closely related to this statue and documented only recently, exist in a private European and North American collection.

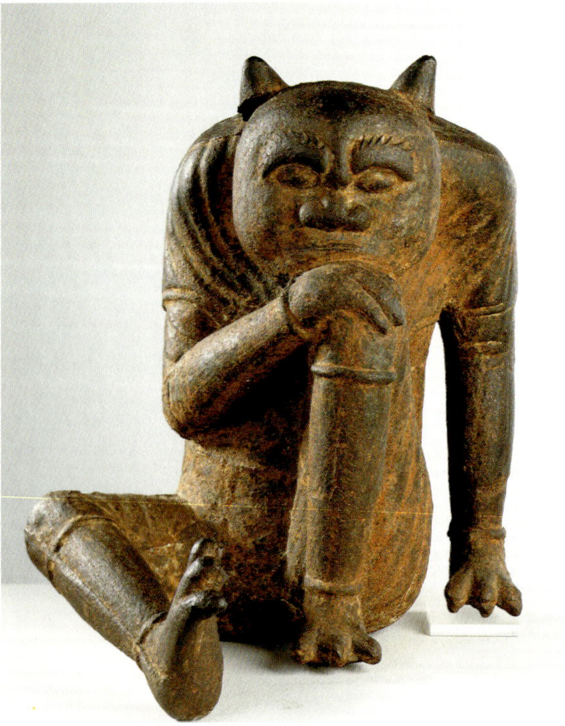

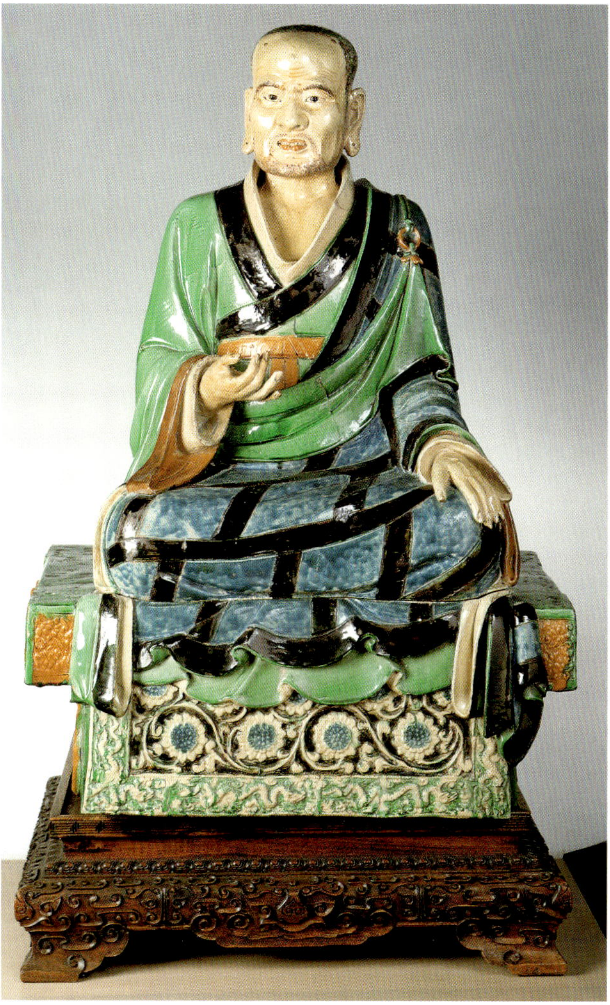

Seated Arhat (*Luohan*)

Ming dynasty, 16th century
Light grey clay with coloured glazes
Height (without base) 94 cm
Inv. No. 1959-3

The Arhat (C: *Luohan*) dressed in Buddhist priest's robes sits with his legs folded under him on a base draped with a cloth bordered with dragons and flowering vines. While the reconstructed right hand is held upright, the left hand rests on the knee. An "Arhat" is a Buddhist disciple or saint who through strict asceticism is able to reach enlightenment, thus releasing himself from the cycle of rebirth. These figures were especially revered by Chan (J: Zen) Buddhist monks. In China they were assembled into groups of sixteen and, later, eighteen or 500. This figure belongs to a series of sixteen or eighteen Arhats, arranged in a row along the walls of the central hall in a Chinese temple.

Mandarins and Persimmons

Nanjing, Jiangsu province
Ming dynasty, 1633
Colour woodblock print from the "Ten Bamboo Studio"
27.3 x 28.3 cm
Inv. No. 6408-27.81

The *Treatise on the Paintings and Writings of the Ten Bamboo Studio* (C: *Shizhuzhai shuhua pu*), published in 1633 in sixteen volumes, is one of the most impressive works of Chinese woodblock prints. The scholar Hu Zhengyan (ca. 1582–1672), who had many artistic talents and chose the name "Ten Bamboo Studio" for his print workshop, produced this collection over the course of several years in collaboration with a team of more than thirty painters and calligraphers. The compendium was to serve as a guide to emerging artists and provide inspiration and enjoyment for experienced artists and art lovers. The collection is divided into eight sections, with two volumes dedicated to each section. Thematically, it focuses on the genre of flower and bird painting. The collection at the Museum contains 128 illustrations from the first edition. In 1927 these illustrations and four other volumes of the *Mustard Seed Garden Painting Manual* (C: *Jieziyuan huazhuan*), a guide to painting published between 1679 and 1701, were added to the collection of the Berlin Art Library, which was responsible at the time for East Asian prints in state collections and was incorporated into the Museum of East Asian Art in 1967. The print shown here is taken from a monograph dedicated to fruit. It is a splendid example of the highly developed art of colour woodblock printing using several printing blocks.

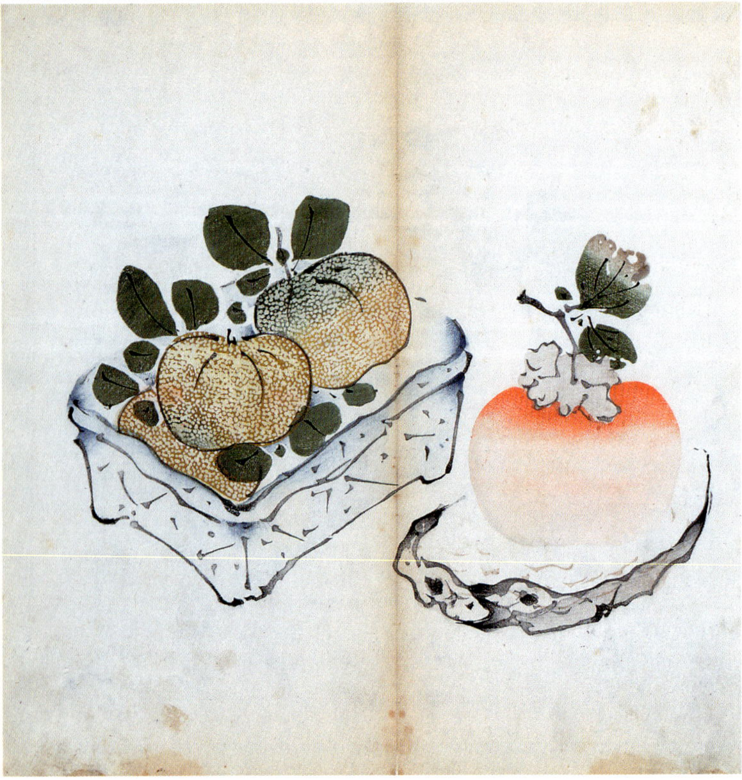

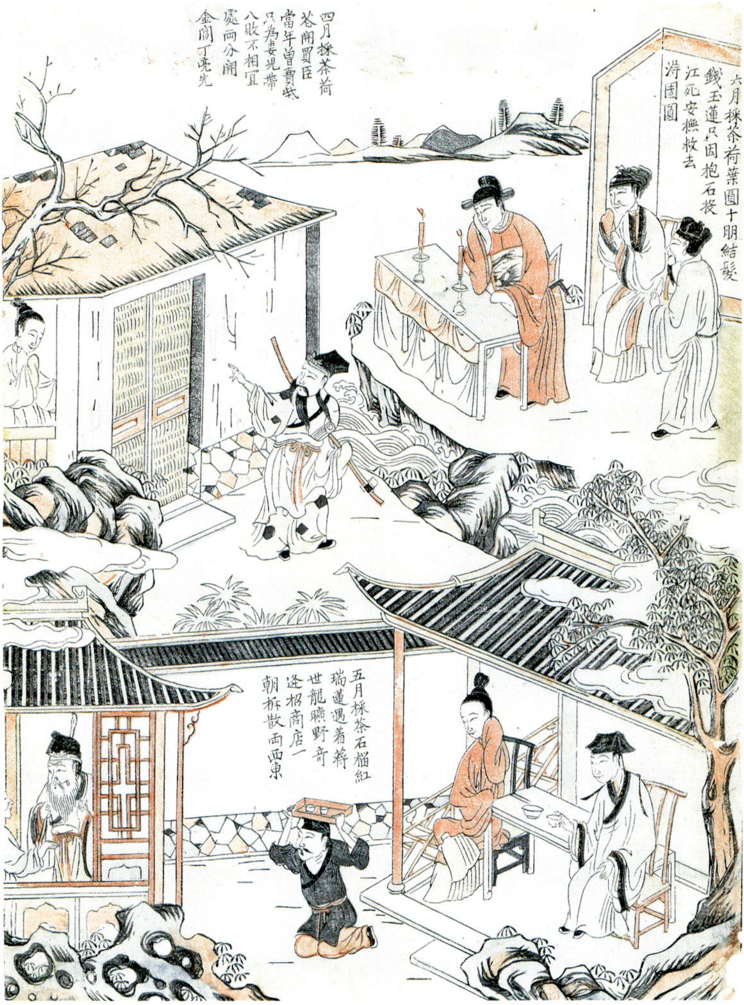

The method of carving a separate woodblock for each colour was invented in the late Ming dynasty. As many as eight separate blocks were used for some of the prints in the *Ten Bamboo Studio* series.

Woodblock illustration is an ancient tradition in China, dating back over a thousand years. The oldest preserved print is the illustration of a Buddhist teaching text from 868 (now in the British Museum, London).

Ding Liangxian
Calendar leaf: illustration of fourth to sixth month

Suzhou, Jiangsu province
Qing dynasty, second half of 17th century
Colour woodblock print
33.4 x 25.7 cm
Inv. No. 1984-12

Among the most renowned printing and publishing houses in Suzhou was that of the Ding family. Prints originating from this workshop are among the most coveted treasures in collections of Chinese graphics. The so-called "Kaempfer prints" – exquisite late-17th-century colour woodblock prints from this workshop – have become especially famous. The Berlin Collection is fortunate to contain two such exhibits. These prints are named after Engelbert Kaempfer (1651–1716), a German physician in Dutch employ who acquired late-17th-century Chinese colour woodblock prints in Nagasaki between 1690 and 1692. These works are astonishing for their outstanding technical quality, the undiminished luminosity of their colours, and the subtlety of the colour gradation. Also from the Ding workshop are two series of calendar sheets with a richly gradated colour palette, here illustrated in one example of a series of four sheets of images of the months, acquired for the collection in 1984. An additional print from the series with images that symbolize the four seasons, in this case summer, was acquired in 1990. A nearly complete sequence of both series is contained in the State Collection of Graphic Arts in Munich.

In addition to the black contour lines, up to eight colours were used for these prints. The calendar leaf shows illustrations for the fourth to sixth month, set into the image by means of figurative, anecdotal depictions in a landscape context and annotated with accompanying poems. The image for the fourth month can be seen on the upper left, that of the fifth month on the bottom left and the last for the sixth month on the upper right. The signature appears at the end of the first poem: "[made] by Ding Liangxian at Jinchang pavilion [in Suzhou]." The individual scenes are separated by the walls of an estate or cliffs against which waves and ocean spray are breaking. The scenes are drawn from an abundance of anecdotes. Thus the scene on the upper left, the fourth month, depicts a man carrying a hoe, his brow furrowed as he takes leave from a woman who sadly watches his departure the window of a humble abode. The accompanying poem explains the scene:

The lotus flowers in the fourth month.
Once upon a time Mai Chen carried firewood for sale.
Because his wife bestowed her favours on others all too freely,
The couple went their separate ways.

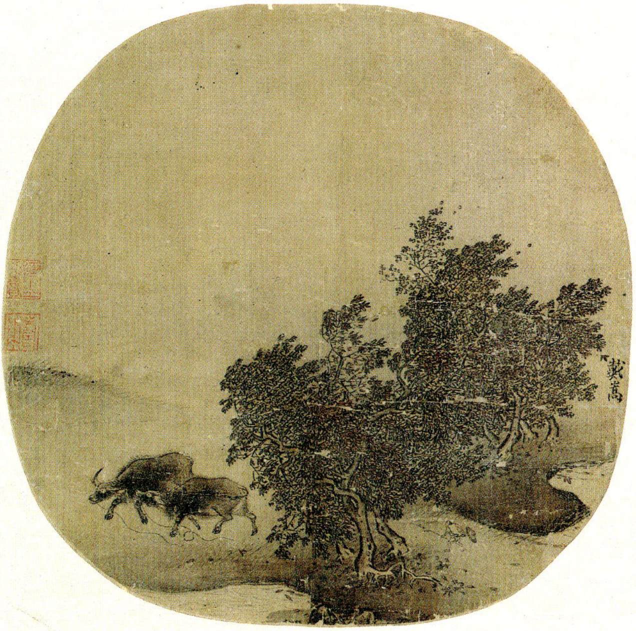

Anonymous
"Water Buffaloes under Autumn Trees"

Song dynasty, 12th–13th century
Fan, ink and colours on silk
Height 23.8 cm, width 25.3 cm
Inv. No. 206-7

On the right side the fan bears the signature of the painter Dai Song from the 8th century, renowned for his images of water buffaloes. However, the signature was added later to give this picture greater stature. In composition and style this work is identified as dating from the Southern Song dynasty (1127–1279).

Fan paintings on the subject of landscapes with water buffaloes were especially popular during the Southern Song dynasty. Water buffaloes were depicted in Chinese painting as early as the Han dynasty, but only in the Northern Song dynasty did they become an autonomous theme. The fan shows two water buffaloes, dragging their reins behind them as they rush towards the stable in the face of an oncoming storm. Early red autumn leaves are already falling from the trees; the cowherd hastens after the animals in his charge, walking stick in hand, his straw hat having just been swept off his head. "Water Buffaloes under Autumn Trees" seems to present a pastoral idyll to the viewer; however, a number of alternate interpretations are also possible, such as Daoist, Confucian, or Chan-Buddhist ones. The format of the round fan suggests a genre scene. The composition, complete within itself with the diagonal spatial division typical of the Southern Song dynasty, indicates that this small masterpiece was conceived as a fan.

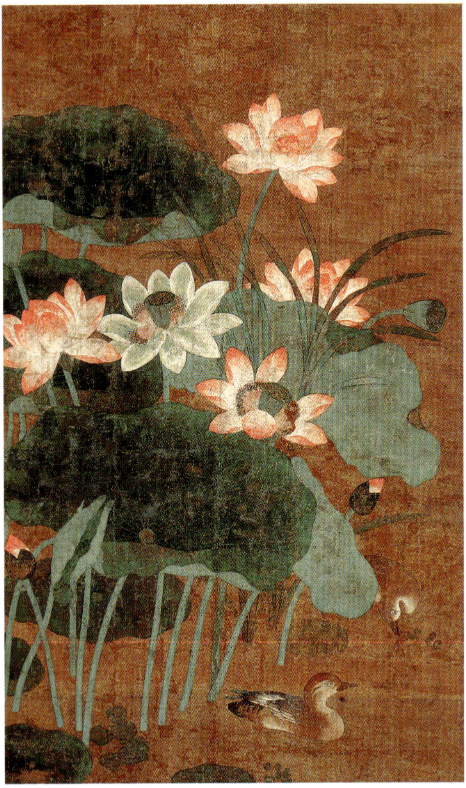

Anonymous

"Ducks in Lotus Pond"
Yuan dynasty, 13th–14th century
Hanging scroll, ink and colour on silk
Height 128 cm, width 78 cm
Inv. No. 5808
Ernst Große Estate

In a pond a pair of ducks swims in the shade of broad lotus leaves. The red and white lotus blossoms are depicted in all stages of opening buds, full flowering, and wilted blossoms. A seed pod is bending towards the right margin. The tender red and white of the flowers and the opaque green of the broad leaves contrast sharply with the silk base, darkened with age.

This summer scene was most likely the left half of a pair of hanging scrolls. Originally created as works in the category of "flower and bird painting," images of this type were later used in Buddhist temples and monasteries. The lotus plays an important role in Buddhist symbolism; thus, Buddhas and Bodhisattvas are seated on lotus thrones. The Bodhisattva Avalokitesvara, for example, is often depicted holding a lotus flower. The lotus grows in murky water, yet dazzles with its immaculate purity.

Lotus images of this kind were created by professional painters. In Piling, a city in Jiangsu province, one particular workshop during the Song and Yuan dynasties specialized for several generations in lotus images.

Whether such lotus images had a Buddhist connotation at the time of their creation is unclear, since none have been preserved in China. Early on, however, lotus paintings reached Japan, where they were carefully preserved in Buddhist temples for centuries. This scroll was acquired by Ernst Große (1862–1927) in Japan. A thematically related scroll, also attributed to the Piling workshop, is housed in the Museum of East Asian Art, Cologne.

The elaborate mounting of the hanging scroll with gold-threaded silk brocade and gilt copper finials on the roller identify this scroll as a sacred image from a Japanese Buddhist temple. The scroll was remounted some twenty-five years ago in Japan following traditional models.

Wang Yuan
"Bamboo, Rock, and Pair of Ducks"

Yuan dynasty, dated 1347
Hanging scroll,
ink on paper
Height 130 cm,
width 55 cm
Inv. No. 1966-37

Inscription: *Painted by Wang Yuan Ruoshui of Qiantang in the dinghai-year of the Zhizheng era* [1347].

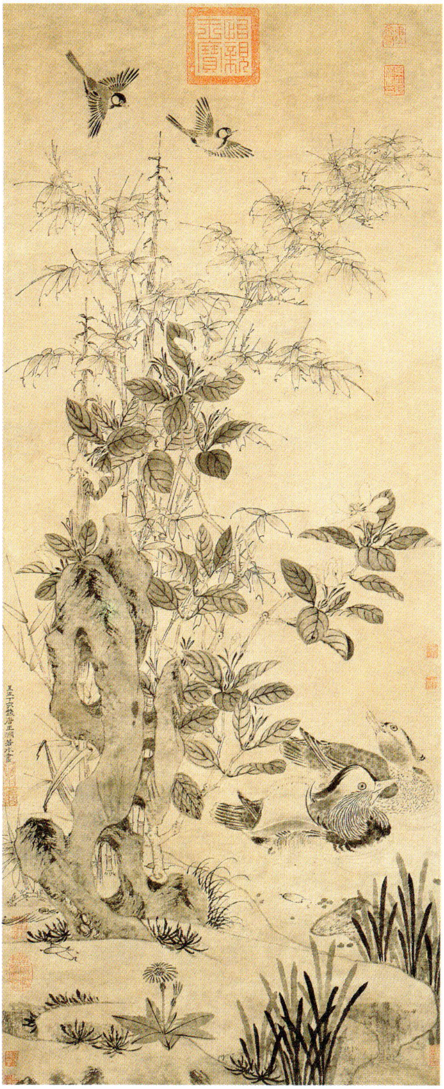

The biographical data of the painter Wang Yuan are not known. Circa 1328 he is said to have executed murals in a palace and a Buddhist temple. All his recorded paintings date from the 1340s. Wang Yuan was a student of Zhao Mengfu (1254–1322), the foremost calligrapher of the Yuan dynasty and a highly innovative and versatile painter. His work is closely related to the traditional style of the Song dynasty with naturalistic colour depictions of birds and flowers on silk, and owes even more to literati painting in ink on paper.

This painting shows a bizarrely shaped garden rock, half-obscuring a gardenia bush and a bamboo in the background. The flowering gardenia, the pair of mandarin ducks floating beneath, and especially the young bamboo, reaching nearly to the top edge of the image, around which two starlings flutter, mark this as a spring image.

The artist uses a variety of brush techniques: precise contour lines that match the elegant clerical script of his signature alternate with washes that give the rock volume and substance.

The large seal at the upper margin indicates that the scroll was in the possession of the second Prince Yi (d. 1798) in the second half of the 18th century, a grandson of Emperor Kangxi (r. 1662–1722).

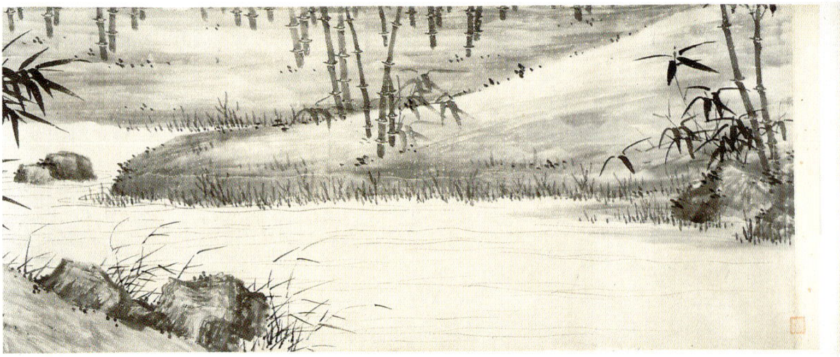

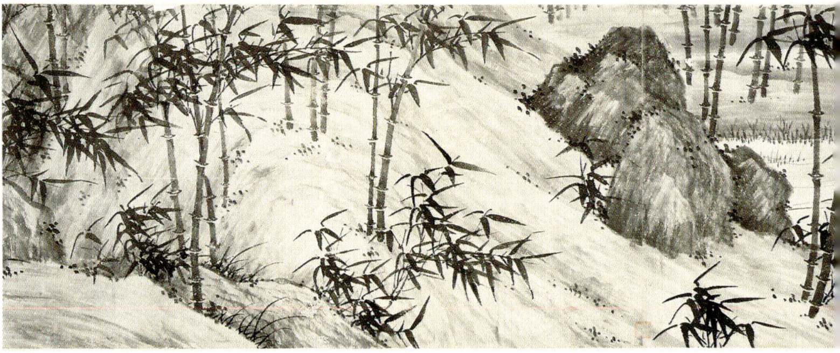

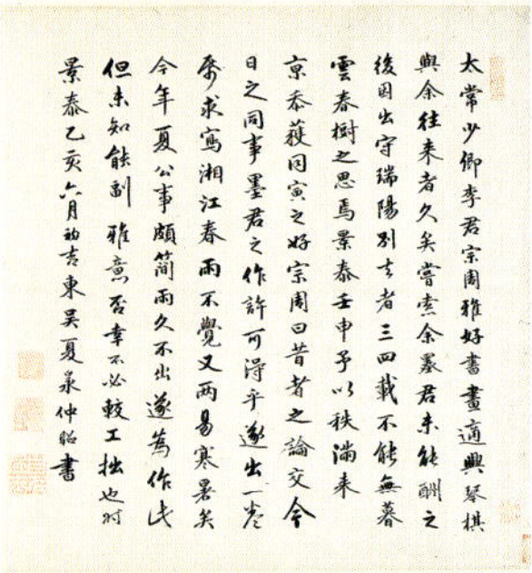

太常少卿李君宗周雅好書畫適興琴棋
與余往来者久矣嘗索余墨君未能酬之
後因出守瑞陽别去者三四載不能無暮
雲春樹之思焉景泰壬申予以秩滿来
京忝蒞同寅之好宗周曰昔者之論交今
日之同事墨君之作許可得乎遂出一卷
索求寫湘江春雨不覺又兩易寒暑矣
今年夏公事頗簡雨久不出遂為作此
但未知能副雅意否幸不必較工拙也时
景泰乙亥六月初吉東吳夏昶仲昭書

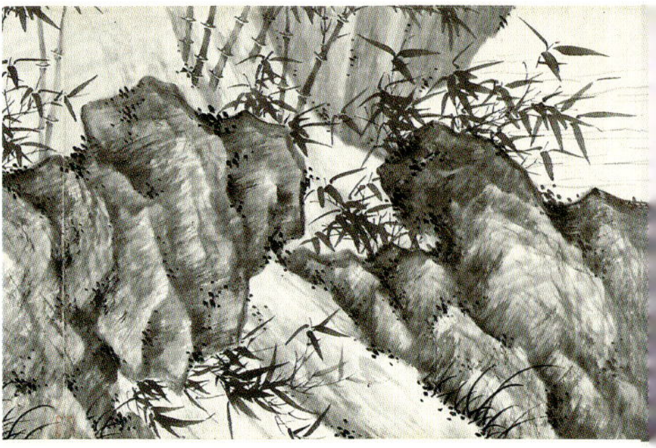

Xia Chang (1388–1470)
"Spring Rain over the Xiang River"

Ming dynasty, dated 1455
Handscroll, ink on paper
Height 44.5 cm, width 900 cm
Inv. No. 5332

This monumental handscroll with six extensive colophons tells in image and word of the historic importance of bamboo in China. The title calligraphy by the high official Ren Daoxun (1422–1503) informs the viewer in a powerful standard script of the contents of the scroll about to unfold: "Spring Rain over the Xiang River." The region of the Xiang River in today's Hunan province has long been famous for its bamboo. Many legends are linked to this plant that stays green all winter, a symbol in China of an upright and noble man, but also, together with the pine and the winter plum, a symbol of long life.

On a 9-metre handscroll, the painter illustrates the riverbanks of

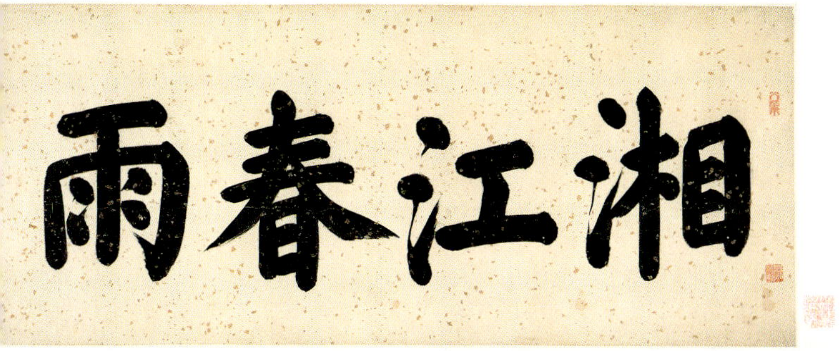

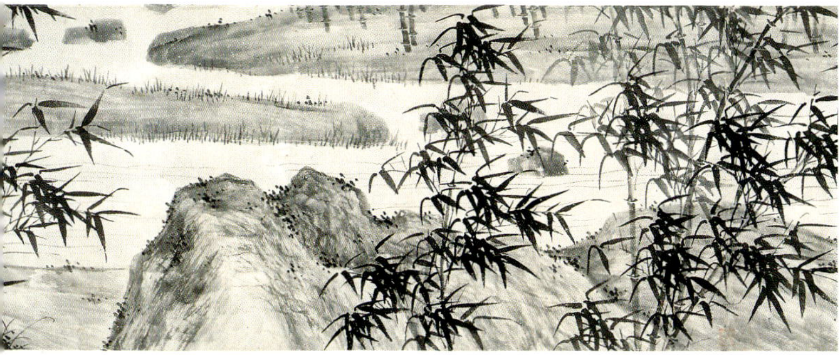

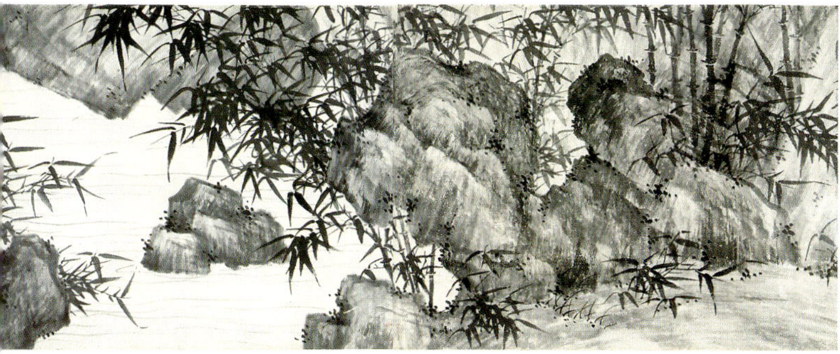

the Xiang with dense bamboo growth and rocks. As if travelling on a riverboat, the viewer sees only a segment of the landscape gliding past through a narrow open window. This composition is typical of the early Ming dynasty.

When Xia Chang painted this image, he had already risen to the position of vice minister of the imperial ritual office. As is evident in the postscript by the artist, the scroll was painted for a colleague. The early Ming dynasty saw a new orientation in Chinese painting with the first division of painting into professional painting, later referred to as the Zhe school, and literati or academic painting, called the Wu school.

Xia Chang is considered one of the foremost calligraphers of his day, especially of standard script. Mastering this type of script was regarded as a prerequisite to bamboo painting, an autonomous genre since the Song dynasty.

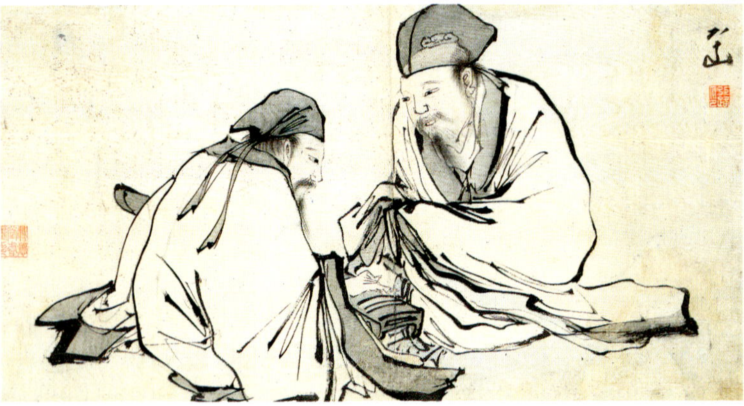

Zhang Lu (ca. 1490 to ca. 1563)
"Playing the Zither for a Friend"

Ming dynasty, first half of 16th century
Album leaf, mounted as hanging scroll
Ink and light colour on silk
Height 31.4 cm, width 61 cm
Inv. No. 1992-20

With the large-format album leaf "Playing the Zither for a Friend" by Zhang Lu, mounted as a hanging scroll, and the handscroll "Four Landscapes" by Jiang Song (first half of 16th century), the Museum possesses two representative works of the Zhe school, exemplary documents of landscape and figure painting. The Zhe school, which included the court and professional painters of the Ming dynasty, is the counterpart to the Wu school, to which the literati painters (amateur scholars and officials) belonged. While the Wu school of painting was highly appreciated, the painting of the Zhe school was regarded as technically brilliant but inferior in artistic spirit, from the late Ming dynasty onwards.

Zhang Lu hailed from Kaifeng, the capital of the Northern Song dynasty, and was revered as one of the great painters of the north during his lifetime. From a wealthy family, he abandoned a career as a civil servant, and retreated into seclusion to pursue the art of painting. He modelled his work on the art of Wu Wei (1459–1508), a painter known for his expressive, rapid, and masterly brush technique. Wu Wei is one of the leading painters of the early Zhe school.

Zhang Lu's best works are said to date from his early creative period. He is especially admired in the literature for his masterful brushwork in figure paintings. With rapid and varied brushstrokes he describes the folds in robes, some of his lines being "as fine as a spider's web."

This image depicts two seated scholars facing each other. One is playing the zither, while the other listens attentively. A profound, almost intimate understanding can be felt between the player and the listener. This spiritual closeness is also expressed in the compact composition, further enhanced by the intensified gathering of the folds in the centre of the image.

The viewer is reminded of the well-known tale of Boya, a scholar from the Zhou era, whose zither-playing was understood only by Zhong Ziqi, a woodcutter. Zhong understood Boya's thoughts, which he was trying to express in his music. When Zhong died, Boya broke his instrument since no one would now understand his music.

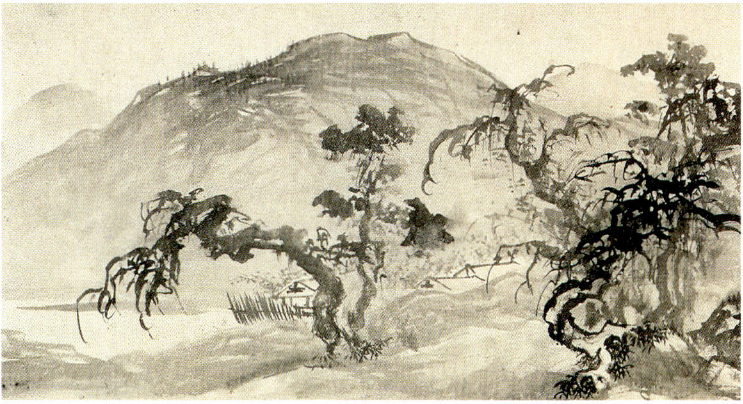

Jiang Song
(active during the early 16th century)
Landscape (detail)

Ming dynasty, first half of 16th century
Handscroll, ink on paper
Height 23 cm
Inv. No. 1372
Donated by Carl Hohn

Like Zhang Lu, Jiang Song belonged among the heterodox painters of the second half of the Ming dynasty. Revered in his lifetime, his art was forgotten after his death, or rather it was reviled because it was classified as being outside of established rules. As was the case for the artists of the Zhe school, Jiang Song suffered from the stigma of the professional painter, although not a few scholars also made their living from the sale of paintings and Jiang came from a long line of scholars. This strict and judgmental division into literati and professional painting occurred only in the late Ming dynasty.

The detail shows the first of four landscapes on a handscroll, of which only the last is signed by the artist while the others merely bear his seal. Jiang Song's well-known oeuvre consists mostly of large hanging scrolls on a limited theme and composition, with the exception of a few smaller works. The images are remarkable for their strong atmospheric impact and the virtuosity of the brushwork, often too much in the foreground. Jiang Song's work was described by later critics as too facile and decorative.

This handscroll is one of the painter's most beautiful and exciting paintings; in it, he turned his back completely on the style of the literati school. Using a masterful and free brush technique, he created four highly distinct landscapes that are deeply moving. He employed washes in a truly masterful manner next to deep, black brushstrokes of almost unfettered freedom, whose impact he heightened by means of so-called "burnt" ink. "Burnt" ink is the name given to ink whose appearance on paper is very dry, almost grainy, as if the lines had been drawn with a thick charcoal stick instead of a brush.

This scroll was acquired as early as 1909 by Ernst Große in Beijing. It is one of the earliest important acquisitions in China of Ming-dynasty paintings for a German collection. Prior to 1909, the main sources had been the Japanese art dealer Hayashi Tadamasa (1853–1906) in Paris and art dealers in Japan.

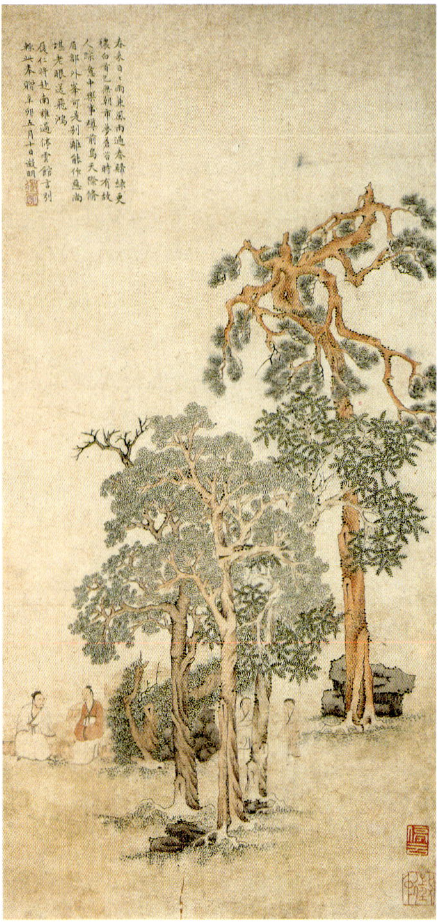

Wen Zhengming (1470–1559)
"Farewell at Tingyunguan"

Ming dynasty, dated May 25, 1531
Hanging scroll, ink and colour on paper
Height 52 cm, width 25.7 cm
Inv. No. 1988-446
Formerly Mochan shanzhuang Collection

Inscription:
Spring approaches and day after day it rains and storms.
After the rains, spring recedes and the green is even more lush.
White-haired, I no longer dream of high office.
From time to time on the green moss are the footsteps of old friends.
The bird in front of the wine jug is the joy of my heart.
The peaks beyond the city walls, long eyebrows on the horizon.
'Tis true, farewell brings sorrow!
How painful for these old eyes to watch the wild geese flying away.

Lüren [Wang Chong, 1494–1533] *was on his way to Nanyong* [Nanjing] *and passed* [by my estate] *Tingyunguan to bid farewell. So I give him* [this picture]. *The 10th day of the 5th month in the xinmao-year. Zheng Ming.*

With his teacher, Shen Zhou (1427–1509), Wen Zhengming is considered the founder of the Wu school, the Ming-dynasty school of literati painting. Wu is the name of the region that surrounds the city of Suzhou, Jiangsu province, the cultural centre of the Ming dynasty. From an old family of scholars, Wen Zhengming was a leading personality in the literary society of Suzhou. This small farewell image is an eloquent testimony to the deep friendship between Wen Zhengming and Wang Chong, younger by twenty-four years, whom he appreciated as a talented poet and calligrapher. The use of trees and rock without fore- or background evokes the serene, pure atmosphere of a scholar's garden. The friends are seated on a rock at the edge of the image, engaged in conversation. Two servants await their command. Unpretentiously and in delicate colours, Wen Zhengming demonstrates the calligraphic style of painting of the literati school, here in the style of the small standard script, analogous to his poem in the upper corner. The last two lines seem to express a premonition of Wang Chong's fate. A mere two years later, Weng Zhengming had to compose an epitaph for his young friend.

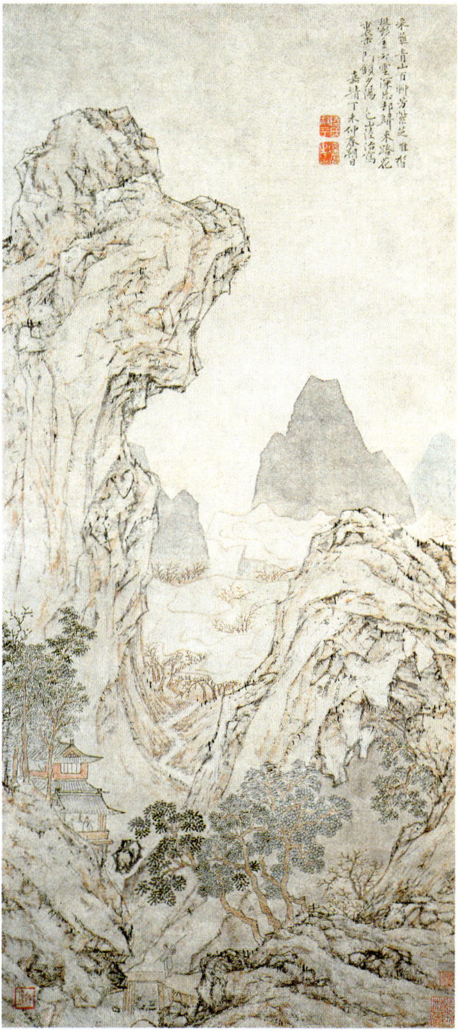

Lu Zhi (1496–1576)
"Gathering Herbs in the Mountains"

Ming dynasty, dated February 20, 1547
Hanging scroll
Ink and colour on paper
70.8 x 32.9 cm
Inv. No. 1988-424
Formerly Mochan shanzhuang Collection

Inscription:
Gathering herbs in the
mountains, aroma
of a hundred plants.
Violet mushrooms
abound! Turmeric
disperses its scent.
Clouds gather, the path
home is forgotten.
The evening sun is held
within the flowers,
tightly closed.

Written [by] *Lu Zhi* [and his given name] *Baoshan on the first day of the second month of spring of the dingwei-year* [February 20, 1547] *of the Jiajing era* [1522–1566].

Lu Zhi is considered one of the most important artists of the 16th century. He was from Suzhou, Jiangsu province, and received an education that prepared him for public service. He took the provincial examinations several times but failed to pass, whereupon he retreated into a life of solitude at the foot of the Zhixing mountain outside of Suzhou, near the shores of Lake Taihu.

Characteristic elements of Lu Zhi's painting are his delicate colour palette, with a light earth tone predominating, and his unique, dry brushstroke with which he creates his characteristic, crystalline mountain and rock formations. In the inscription the viewer's attention is drawn to the herb gatherer in the foreground. The gathering of herbs and Lingzhi mushrooms is a metaphor for the Daoist striving for immortality, retreating from the impurities and dangers of the world into the solitude of the mountains to live in harmony

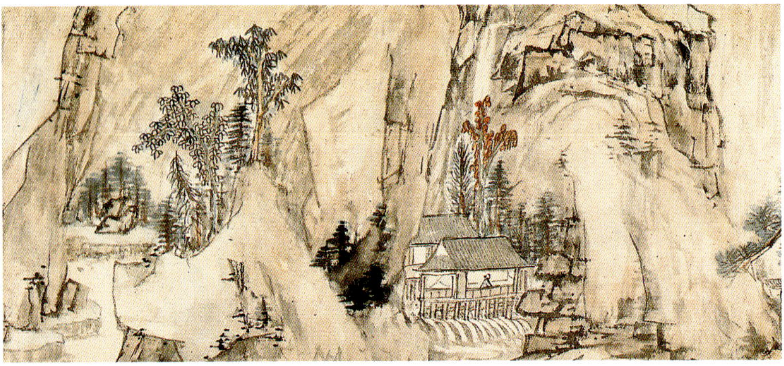

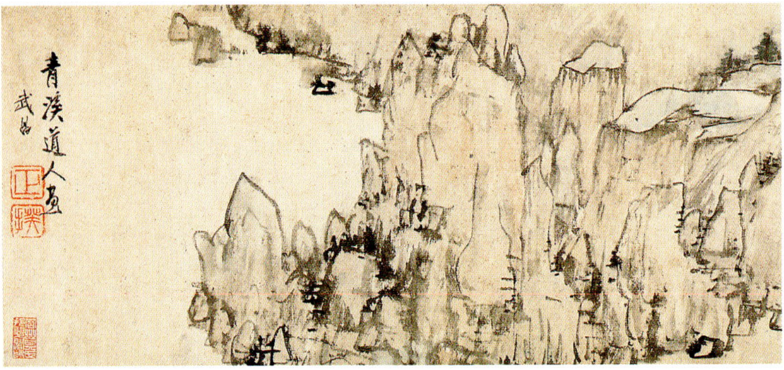

with nature. The cave, a recurring motif in Lu Zhi's oeuvre, is the dwelling of the immortals, but it is also the path into the ideal world. The viewer must decide on which side of the cave he stands.

Cheng Zhengkui (1604–1676)
"Dream Journey among Rivers and Mountains"

Qing dynasty, third quarter of 17th century
Handscroll, ink and colour on paper
Height 22.4 cm, width 205.2 cm
Inv. No. 1988-394
Formerly Mochan shanzhuang Collection

Cheng Zhengkui was a student of Dong Qichang (1555–1636), the artist and art critic, who formulated the theory of dividing Chinese painting into literati and professional painting and whose stylistic innovations breathed new life into Chinese painting. He owned the major work "Dwelling in the Fuchun Mountains" by Huang Gongwang (1269–1354), one of the four great masters of the Yuan dynasty, which Cheng Zhengkui studied at length, as this handscroll documents. Caught up in the turmoil of dynastic change, he joined the new rulers. As a result he was awarded a high position in Beijing and had the leisure to devote himself intensively to painting. This image probably belongs to a series of several hundred with the same title, although the title is not mentioned in the artist's inscription. The preserved images on this theme differ greatly in their manner of painting, composition, and interpretation. So much so, in fact, as to call to mind a statement by Cheng Zhengkui attributed to his teacher Dong Qichang: one could, he said, only begin to paint after one's feet had travelled all the famous mountains of the world and one's eyes had seen all the wondrous paintings by the old masters.

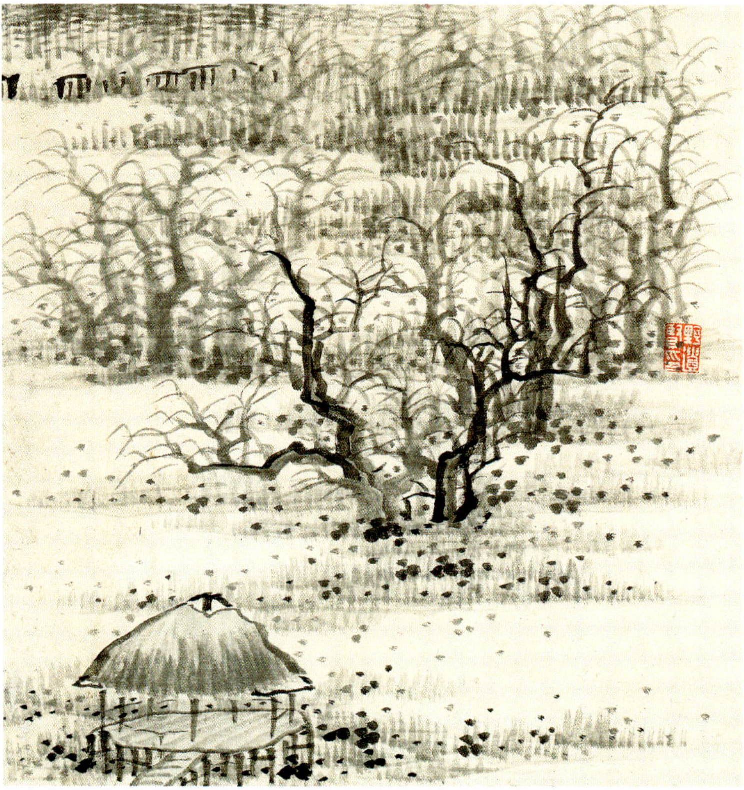

Gong Xian (1619–1689)
"Marsh Landscape"

Qing dynasty, dated 1684
Album leaf, ink on paper
Height 24 cm, width 24.2 cm
Inv. No. 1988-404
Formerly Mochan shanzhuang Collection

Gong Xian is the best known personality of the "Eight Masters from Nanjing," eight painters who lived in the second half of the 17th century in Nanjing. Only a few among this group, however, engaged in an artistic and intellectual exchange.

Gong Xian began to study painting at the early age of twelve. At the beginning of the 1630s, while he was still almost a child, he had the opportunity of studying with Dong Qichang (1555–1636) and his early work betrays the influence of his master's style and theories. The corruption that dominated the late Ming dynasty and the chaos that followed the seizure of power by the Manchu probably instilled a feeling of uncertainty in the young man, and he never sought public office.

With the exception of landscapes or landscape elements, Gong Xian's paintings are devoid of human figures. At times, the human presence is alluded to in a pavilion, or as in this image, in a boat or huts. In contrast to his otherwise extremely dense and complex landscape compositions with a seemingly endless variety in the tonality of ink, he reduced his painterly means in this album leaf to a minimum, achieving what he himself described as "natural and unexpected."

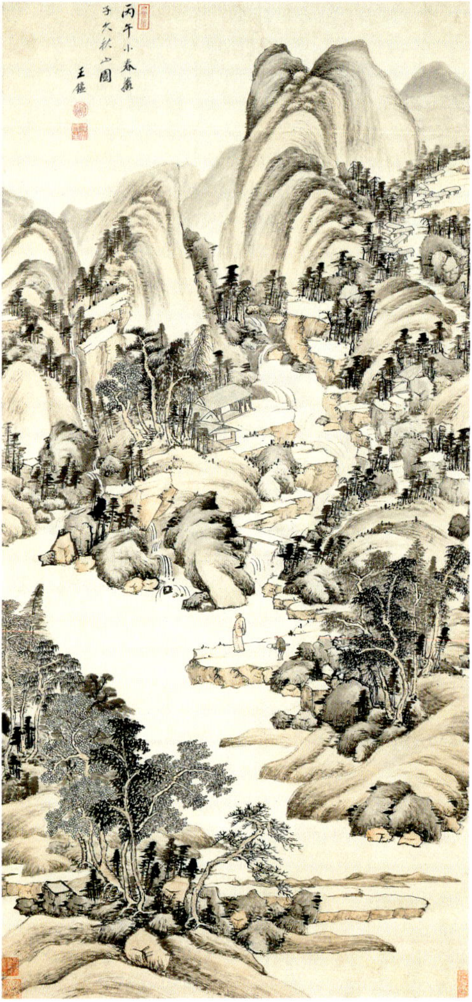

Wang Jian (1598–1677)
"Autumn Mountains in the Style of Huang Gongwang"

Qing dynasty, dated 1666
Hanging scroll, ink and colour on paper
Height 130 cm, width 62.5 cm
Inv. No. 1988-440
Formerly Mochan shanzhuang Collection

Inscription: [I have] *painted the picture "Autumn mountains" in the style of Zijiu in the tenth month of the bingwu-year* [1666]. *Wang Jian.*

Wang Jian hailed from an aristocratic family in Taicang, Jiangsu province. A few years prior to the dynastic change he withdrew from his offices and until his death devoted himself to literature and art. He was strongly influenced by the paintings and theories of Dong Qichang (1555–1636), who was his teacher for several years.

Wang's efforts were made easier by his access to an extensive personal collection of old masters. The new orthodox style of painting, which he promoted, finally gained recognition at the imperial court under his student Wang Hui (1632–1717). In this large hanging scroll, Wang Jian adheres to the compositional ideals of his model Dong. The image is constructed from individual elements, almost in the manner of props whose arrangement invests the painting with a degree of instability. The brushwork betrays a link to Huang Gongwang, as mentioned in the inscription, one of the four great masters of the Yuan dynasty, in whose "hemp-fiber" brushstrokes Shen Zhou (1427–1509) read the expression of rich sensory experiences. To convey the power of nature, Dong Qichang gave the shapes of individual pictorial elements greater autonomy in painting. The beauty of this style reveals itself only in the brushstroke, which is consistent throughout the composition and unifies it. Thus the painter must not only imitate the old masters but nature too, for only then can he create work that will outlive him.

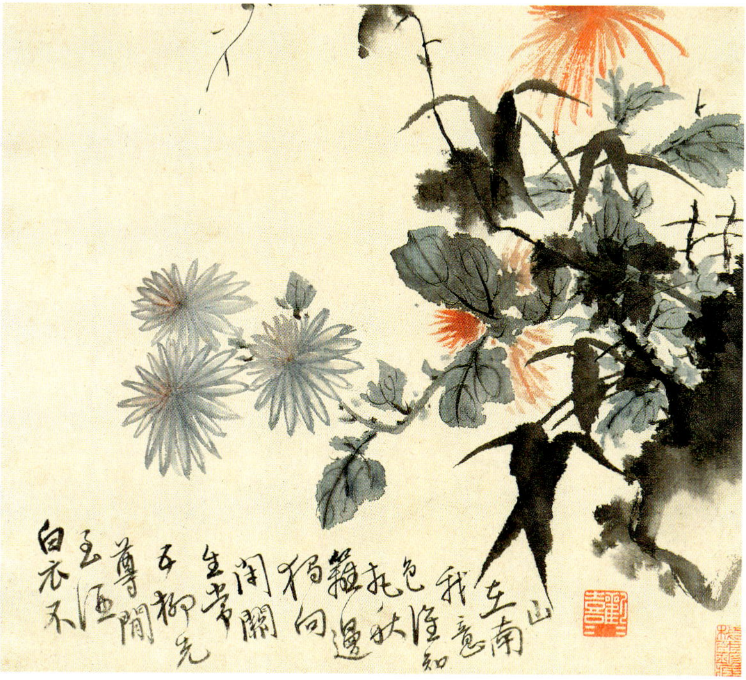

Hua Yan (1682–1756)
"Chrysanthemum, Bamboo, and Rock"

Qing dynasty
Album leaf, ink and colour on paper
Height 31.5 cm, width 36.2 cm
Inv. No. 1988-412
Formerly Mochan shanzhuang Collection

Inscription:
As a simple man I cannot attend official banquets.
The "Master of the Five Willows" withdrew from public life forever.
Alone, leaning against the fence, he held autumn flowers in his hand.
Who understands my yearning for the Southern Mountain?

Hua Yan is considered one of the most talented and versatile artists of the Qing dynasty. His family operated a paper mill in Shanghang, Fujian province, but he settled in Hangzhou early in his life. Apart from a brief sojourn in Beijing, he lived often and for long periods of time in Yangzhou between 1730 and 1752 to earn "clothing and food" for his family.

Yangzhou, one of the wealthiest trade centres in 18th-century China, attracted many artists, who often found support in the homes of affluent salt merchants. One group of these artists is referred to as the "Eight Eccentrics from Yangzhou." Opinions on who the members were vary, and sometimes Hua Yan is counted as belonging to this group.

Script and image harmonize in their cursive execution. In their free and expressive use, ink and colour reflect the content of the poem. Hua Yan identifies the poet Tao Qian (365–427) by his *nom de plume* "Master of the Five Willows" and makes an allusion to his poem entitled "Drinking Wine," which con-

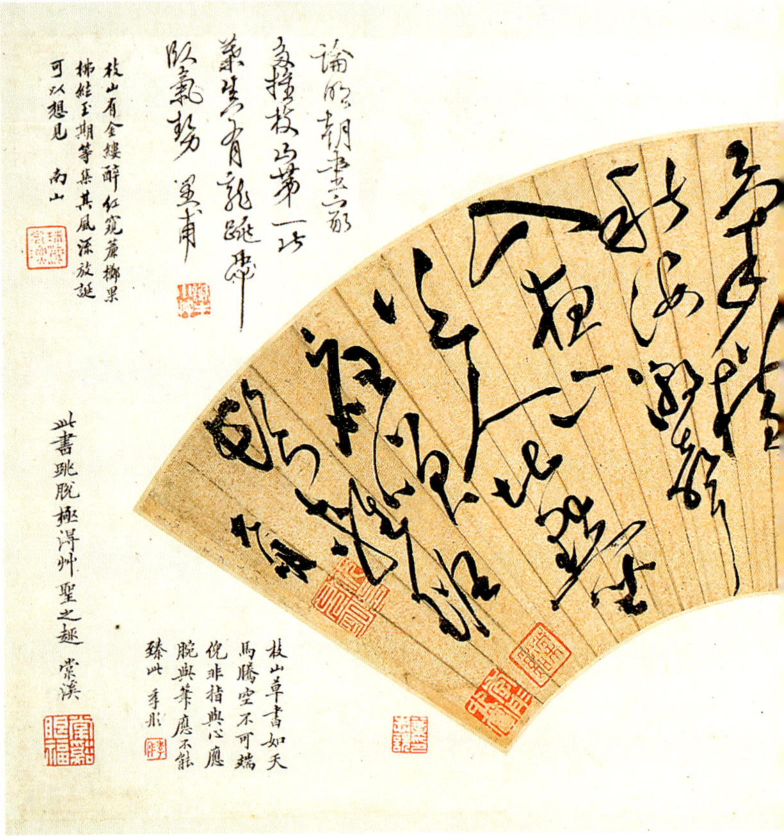

tains the line: "I pluck chrysanthemums at the eastern fence and gaze towards the Southern Mountain." Tao Qian is considered the classic model of the Chinese scholar, who preferred a simple life in the country to a career as an official.

Zhu Yunming (1461–1527)
Poem in draft script

Ming dynasty
Fan, ink on gold-speckled paper
Height 16.5 cm, width 50.1 cm
Inv. No. 1988-389
Formerly Mochan shanzhuang Collection

Inscription:
Overnight in an inn in Qiantang,
Not yet returning at a late hour.
Each place I linger, my mind feels free.
The rains spread over the autumn sea,
At night the sound of the tide is heard in the mountains.
The hermit knows how to sink into the silence,
He should laugh, his temples have already turned grey.

In China, fans were used as a painting surface for calligraphy as early as the 4th century. Since the Ming dynasty, the folding fan has been a popular format for painting and calligraphy.

Zhu Yunming is considered the foremost calligraphy artist of the Ming dynasty. Highly versatile, he was familiar with a number of styles: standard, cursive, and draft script. He

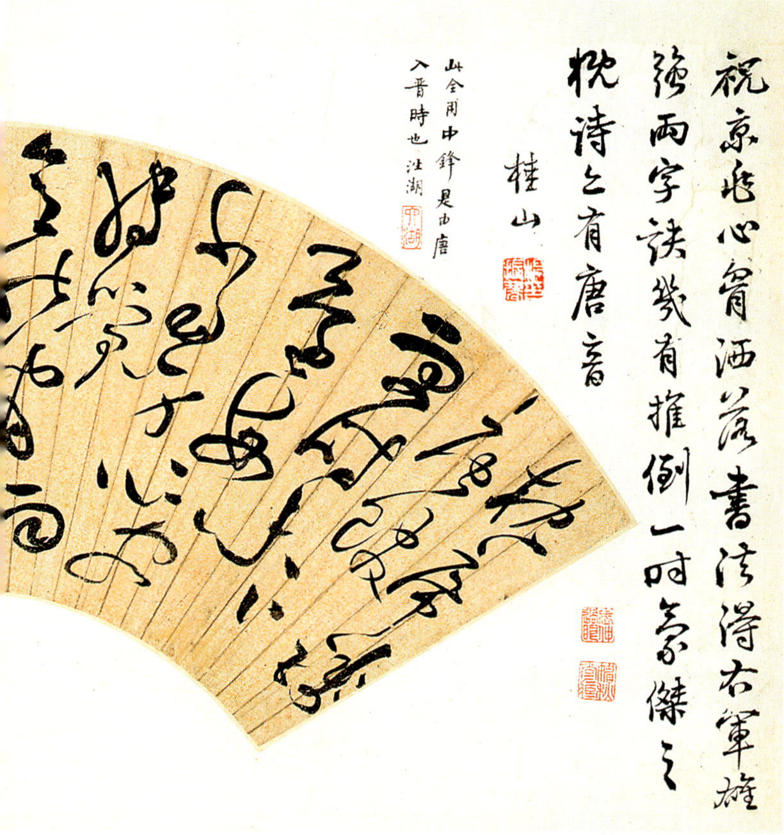

also wrote in the style of many other masters. At an early age he had already benefited from instruction by one of the leading calligraphers in Suzhou, his grandfather Xu Youzhen (state exam 1433). He had access to important collections and was able to study all the great masters. His works in "crazy draft script" were much sought after by his contemporaries. It was based on the work of the monk Huaisu (737–798).

After taking the provincial examination, Zhu Yunming was active as an official only for a short time, after which he preferred to devote himself to his artistic interests.

He was a close friend of Wen Zhengming (1470–1559) and Tang Yin (1470–1527), the two leading personalities of artistic and cultural life in Suzhou. Some critics claim to see his *bon vivant* lifestyle reflected in his seemingly uncontrolled style of calligraphy. In painterly fashion, his brush glides across the paper, the arrangement into calligraphic lines seems to dissolve, parts of individual characters reach far across into adjacent lines, the characters vary in size, and the width of the strokes is highly inconsistent. The result is an image of powerfully rhythmic movement. Zhu himself compares the writing of calligraphy on a folding fan to asking a dancer to demonstrate her art on a heap of broken bricks.

In the accompanying colophons, collectors and connoisseurs of the 18th and 19th centuries compare the calligraphy of this fan to "dancing dragons," "cowering tigers," and even to a "heavenly horse rising into the air."

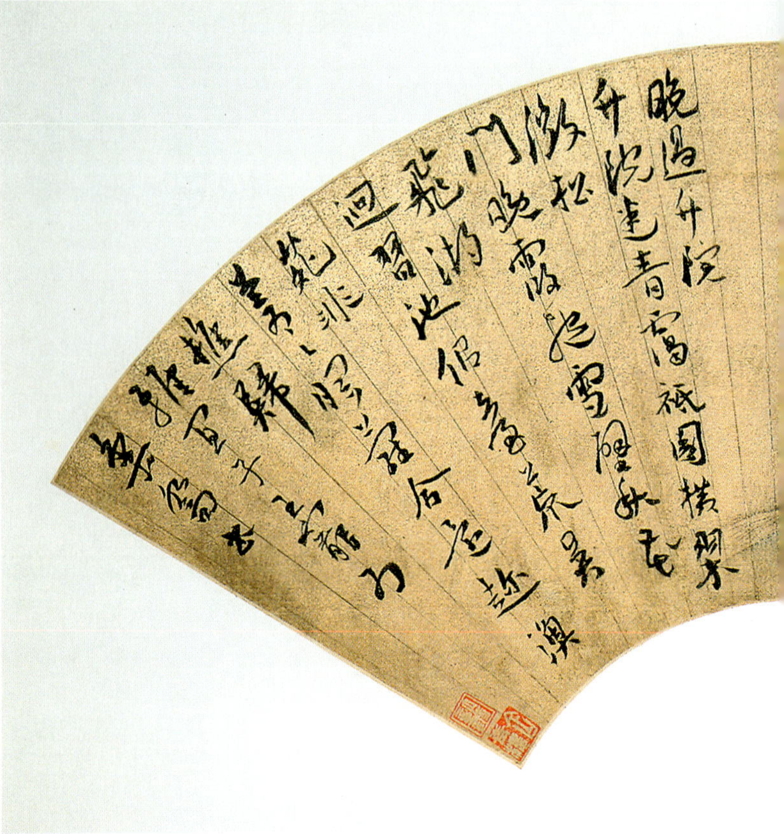

Qiu Ying (d. 1552) painting
Wang Chong (1494–1533) calligraphy
"Visiting a Bamboo Grove in the Evening"
Ming dynasty, ca. 1530
Fan, ink and colour on gold-speckled paper
Height 18.8 cm, width 52.6 cm
Inv. No. 1988-267
Formerly Mochan shanzhuang Collection

Artist's signature: *Painted by Qiu Ying*

Poem: *Visiting a Bamboo Grove in the Evening*

The bamboo grove lies veiled in a pale mist.
The green of the temple garden is soaked with rain
And sunset red surrounds the pine gate.
Autumn flowers sway in front of the snow-white wall.
The curve of the lake's shore surely resembles the Xi pond.
But the overgrown terraces are not the imperial park of Wu.
In the evening dusk, the dark tendrils have fused into one.
The fisherman and the woodcutter are going homewards – I follow them.
Written by Yayizi Wang Chong for Yizhai

Qiu Ying and Wang Chong are among the many artists who lived in Suzhou during the Ming dynasty and who contributed to the city's reputation as China's cultural centre. They were friends with other artists such

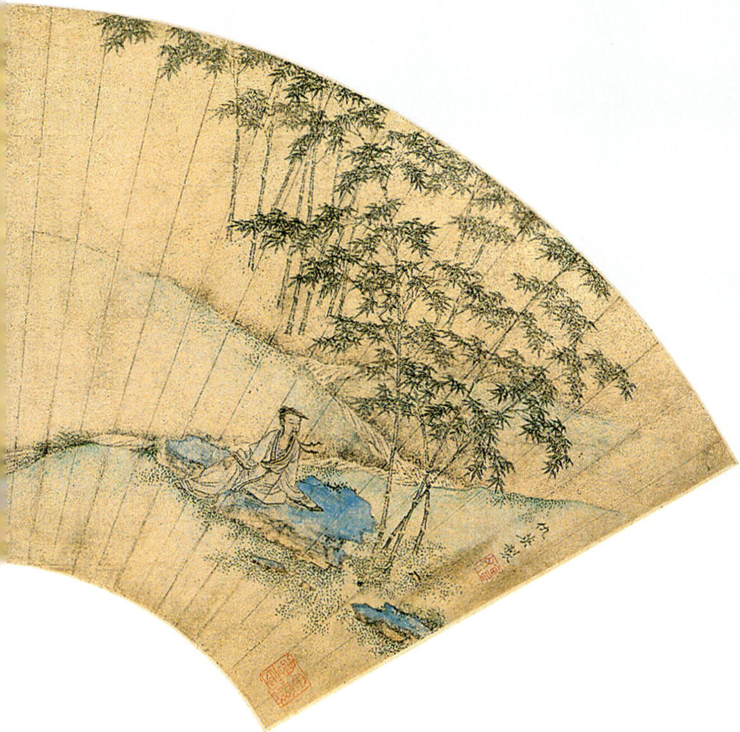

as Wen Zhengming, Zhu Yunming, and Lu Zhi, discussed elsewhere.

Qiu Ying differs from these other artists by virtue of his family background, which did not allow for a classic education. Throughout his life he was a professional painter in high demand, impressing his contemporaries with his technical skill and stylistic versatility.

On this fan, Qiu Ying depicts a scholar seated on a rock in a bamboo grove with characteristically sure, fine brushwork. He uses azurite and malachite, investing the image with an archaic character. Bamboo, rock, and waterfall suggest a garden, a fittingly elegant ambience for a scholar.

Despite his broad knowledge, Wang Chong failed to pass the provincial examination in several attempts; he therefore devoted himself primarily to poetry and calligraphy. His calligraphy is compared to Wen Zhengming's and Zhu Yunming's. It is considered highly cultivated and is regarded as an expression of his flawless, noble character.

In this poem Wang Chong describes what the scholar sees from his perch on the garden rock – but which remains invisible to the viewer in front of the painting – in an elegant, expressive cursive script. Allusions indicate that the "bamboo grove" must have been a garden in Suzhou. The calligraphy places Wang Chong in the tradition of Wang Xizhi (307–367), the patriarch of cursive and draft script, and of Sun Guoting (648?–703?), the foremost proponent of this tradition in the Tang dynasty.

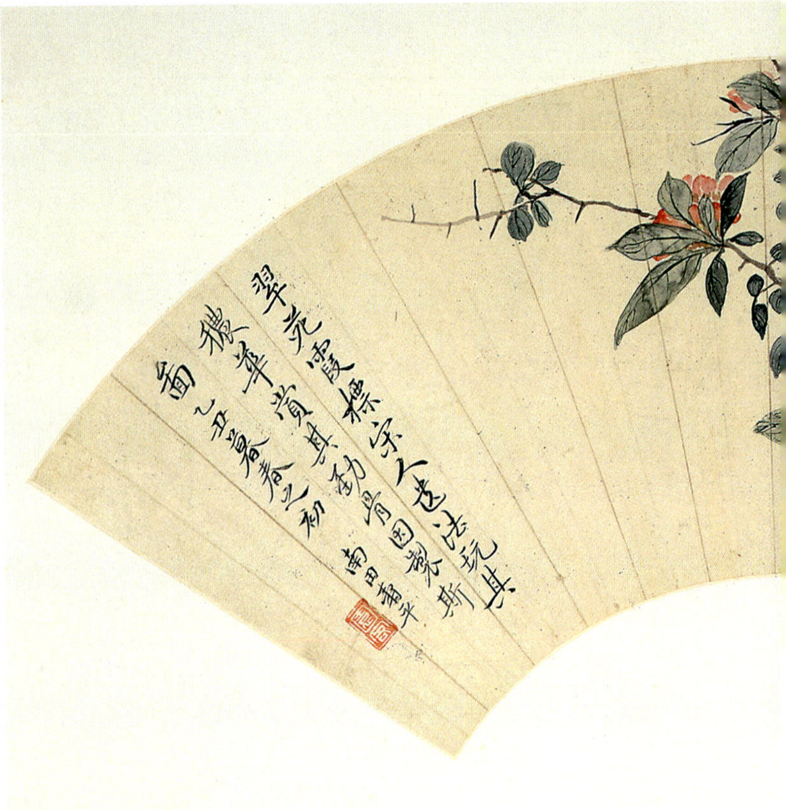

Yun Shouping (1633–1690)
"Flowering Quince"

Qing dynasty, dated 1685
Fan, ink and colour on mica paper
Height 16.9 cm, width 52.1 cm
Inv. No. Dlg. 78-1989
On loan from the Werner-Reimers Foundation, Bad Homburg

Inscription:
Lush green and red blossoms in the tradition handed down by the Song masters.
I have studied their abundance and splendour and value their power and structure.
And so I did this painting at the beginning of late spring in the yichou-year [1685]. Nantian Shouping.

This fan with an image of a flowering quince (*cydonia japonica*) is one of the most beautiful flower paintings in the collection of the Museum. The paper is layered with mica, which enhances the transparency of the colours. As the artist explains in his inscription, he modelled the work on the style of painting practised in the Song dynasty, that is, the style of the imperial academy of the 11th and 12th centuries, which promoted a naturalistic approach in flower and bird painting, relying entirely upon colours and working without ink contours.

Yun Shouping inspired a revival of this genre and had a lasting influence on many painters of the Qing dynasty, notably Hua Yan (1682–1756). As is immediately apparent, Yun Shouping painted from nature, contrary to the conventions of literati

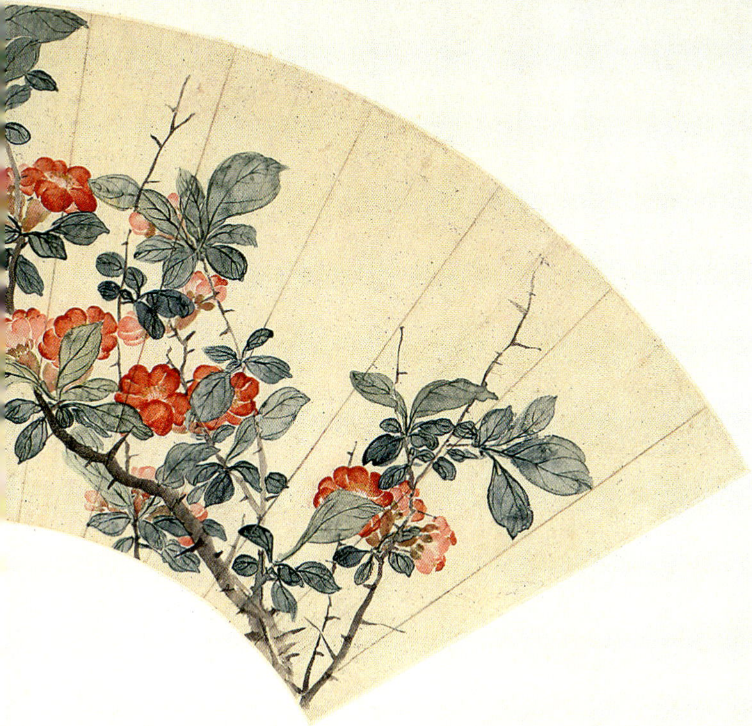

painting. His colours attain a previously unknown transparency. The graphic, linear element is suppressed, without diminishing the artistic calligraphic flow. Calligraphy and painting are in harmony in their delicate yet definitive elegance. The tension in the composition arises as a result of the contrast between the living, flowering branch which grows from the bottom right corner of the fan and spreads across two-thirds of the surface, and the three rigorously arranged lines of characters that form the inscription. As in painting, Yun Shouping developed a personal, unique style in calligraphy.

Yun Shouping was strongly influenced by the dynastic change and the chaotic struggles it entailed. His father was a Ming loyalist and was caught up in the resistance movement against the new rulers. He devoted himself to both landscape and flower painting. An anecdote tells that Yun Shouping focussed on flower painting after he had come to realize that he would never be able to match his friend Wang Hui (1632–1717) in landscape painting. It is more likely that he specialized in the popular theme of "flowers" because he had to support his family through the sale of his paintings. As his family had suffered much from political involvement, he avoided contact with influential officials and civil servants and was constantly dependent on his friends. He died in poverty.

Qi Baishi (1863–1957)
"Eagle on a High Rock"

Republic, dated 1924, 1955 (dedication)
Hanging scroll, ink and colour on paper
Height 263 cm, width 70 cm
Inv. No. OAS 1990-3

Qi Baishi is one of the leading Chinese artists of the 20th century, and certainly the best known in the West. From a humble background, he worked at first as a carpenter, woodcarver, and portrait painter. Only in the second half of his life did he develop a personal style. Qi Baishi is also renowned as a seal carver. His extensive oeuvre, characterized by strong brushwork, includes themes such as flower and bird painting, but he is famous for his innovative depictions of seemingly trivial everyday objects and scenes.

The "Eagle on a High Rock" is an unusual work by this artist. The massive rock, which dominates the monumental format, is integrated into a balanced composition. An animated structure, created by decisive brushstrokes in a broad spectrum of light to dark hues, relieves the block-like character of the columnar monolith. The eagle is perched on top of the rock in a proud and confident pose – in this type of representation a symbol for an independent, noble hero standing on his own and endowed with a sense of justice. On the evidence of the first inscription on the right margin, Qi Baishi created the painting as early as 1924. In 1955 he added a dedication to Otto Grotewohl, then prime minister of the GDR, to whom the painting was presented as a gift. The change in the flow of his calligraphy, set down thirty years later, is clearly evident.

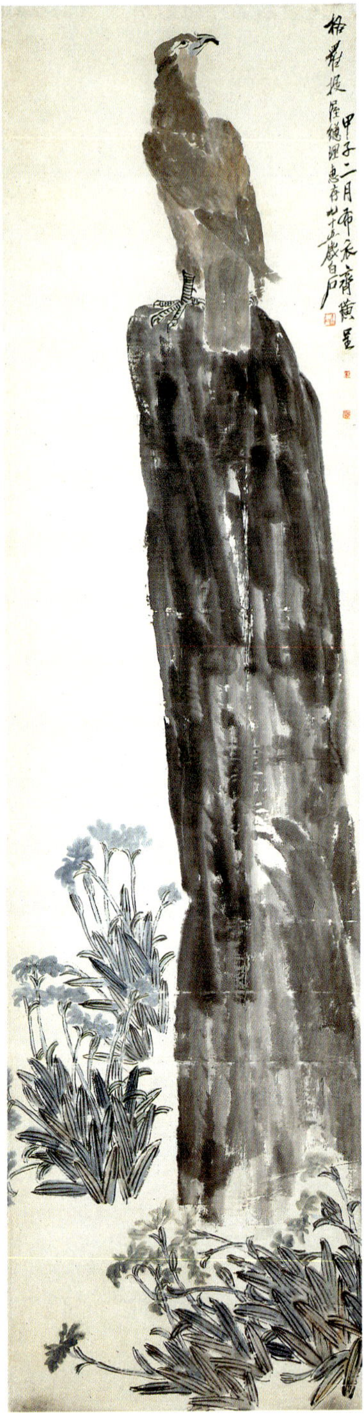

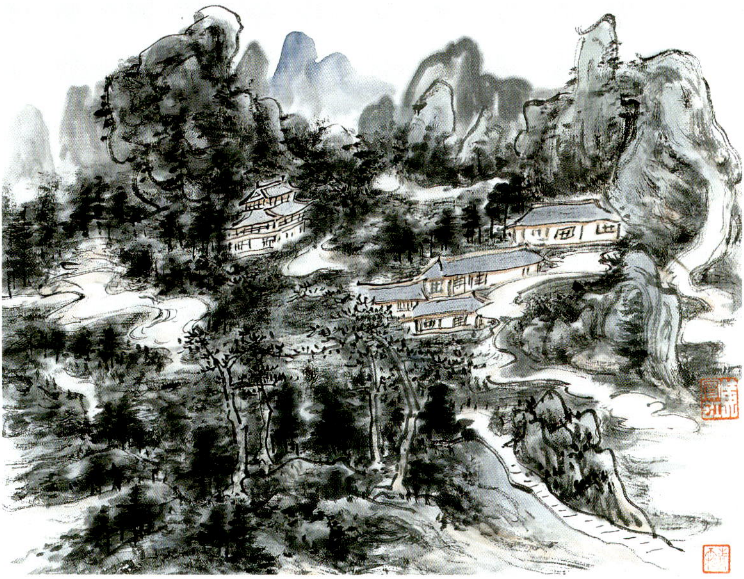

Huang Binhong (1865–1955)
Landscape

People's Republic, dated 1954
Leaf 7 from an album of 8 leaves
Ink and colour on paper
Height 25.9 cm, width 33.6 cm
Inv. No. 1988-77
Formerly Mochan shanzhuang Collection

The compositions of the leaves in this album convey the impressive lushness of the southern Chinese landscapes. Huang Binhong's characteristic style of extremely dense, textured strokes against a background of wet ink and spots of colour reached a peak in this late work. The liberal brushstrokes, at times chaotic in their complexity, display a broad spectrum of finely differentiated gradations. Scattered dwellings, lonely and remote, are the only sign of a human presence in these landscapes, which communicate a sense of the grandeur of nature to the viewer.

From a wealthy family, Huang Binhong benefited from the private education typical of the literati, which also included painting and calligraphy. He is considered the last great master capable of continuing the classic style of ink painting solely on the basis of its tradition and yet able to develop a style all his own. In the course of his long creative career he also distinguished himself as an author of art criticism and an editor of anthologies of classic writings.

Huang Binhong devoted himself primarily to landscape painting. A passionate hiker, he travelled to many different mountain regions in China, favouring especially Huangshan, known for its bizarre rock formations. These mountains had already inspired the painters of the 17th-century Anhui school, in whom he was particularly interested and whose last representative he is sometimes considered to have been. In thousands of sketches Huang Binhong recorded his observations of nature, which had as decisive an influence on his work as his studies of the old masters of the Song and Yuan dynasties.

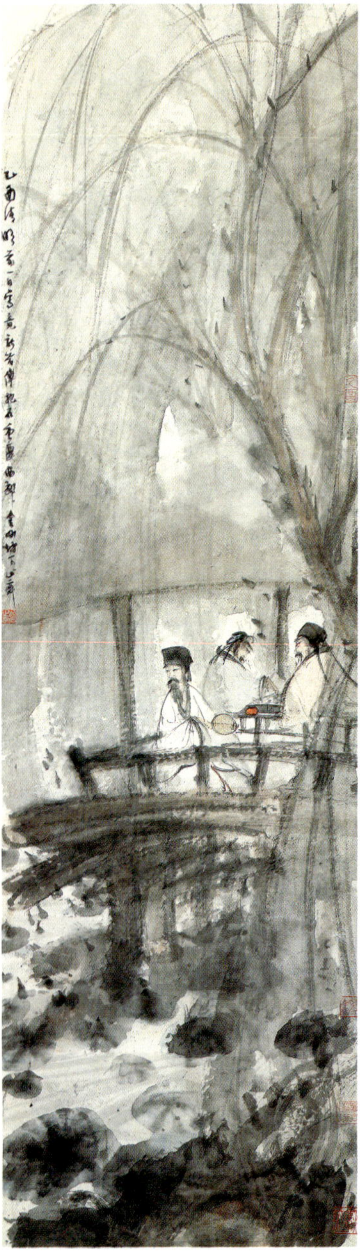

Fu Baoshi (1904–1965)
"Scholars at a Mountain Stream"

Republic, dated 1945
Hanging scroll, ink and colour on paper
Height 137.3 cm, width 40.2 cm
Inv. No. 1988-64
Formerly Mochan shanzhuang Collection

The three scholars enjoy the freshness and cooling shade of a small pavilion set on posts above a mountain stream. Two scholars are engaged in *weiqi*, a board game better known by its Japanese name *go*, while the third seems to be lost in contemplation of nature. In a manner reminiscent of literati painting, Fu Baoshi employs a freer and more individualized style that breaks with the traditional canon.

Sweeping washes give a sense of the moisture rising from the mountain stream. The textured, rapid brushstrokes applied with a dry brush enhance the atmosphere of summery lightness. Only the physiognomy of the scholars and the contours of their robes are clearly outlined with precise brushstrokes against the misty surroundings .

The image is one of a series of similar compositions painted in the mid-1940s, all of which feature three scholars in various elegant leisure pursuits.

Fu Baoshi studied in Japan from 1933 to 1935, where he was strongly influenced not by Japanese painting but by the works of those Chinese artists who were much appreciated in Japan but nearly forgotten in the China of his day. His oeuvre contributed to the rediscovery of these traditional Chinese artists. He was especially inspired by the work of the individualistic monk painter Shitao (1641–1710).

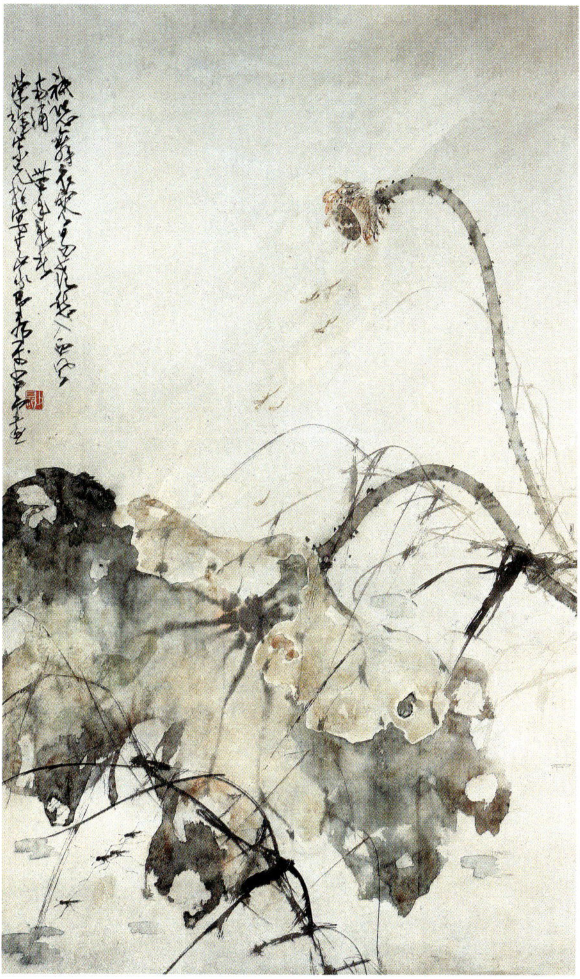

Zhao Shao'ang
(born 1905)
Lotus

Republic, dated 1934
Hanging scroll
Ink and colour on paper
Height 104.8 cm, width 65.1 cm
Inv. No. 1988-173
Formerly Mochan shanzhuang Collection

Bent by the wind, the wilted leaf and seed pod of a lotus at the end of its flowering lean down towards the water. Four precisely rendered pond skaters on the surface of the water seek shelter beneath the enormous leaf which dominates the composition. Masterful colour washes, reminiscent of watercolours, and the absence of contours are characteristic of Zhao Shao'ang's style.

In Buddhism the lotus is a symbol of purity because it blooms above the mud and murky water, which do not adhere to its unique surface. Here, however, the artist – who feels drawn to Chan (J: Zen) Buddhism – reflects on the transitory nature of all things and the vanity of life on earth. Both the inscription and the image are imbued with an undeniably melancholic mood.

Zhao Shao'ang is one of the leading younger representatives of the southern Chinese Lingnan school, which played an avant-garde role, especially in the 1920s and 1930s, in the search for new forms of expression and new subject matter. The adaptation of Western painting techniques, an emphasis on colour, and an interest in modern themes characterize the works of this renewal movement.

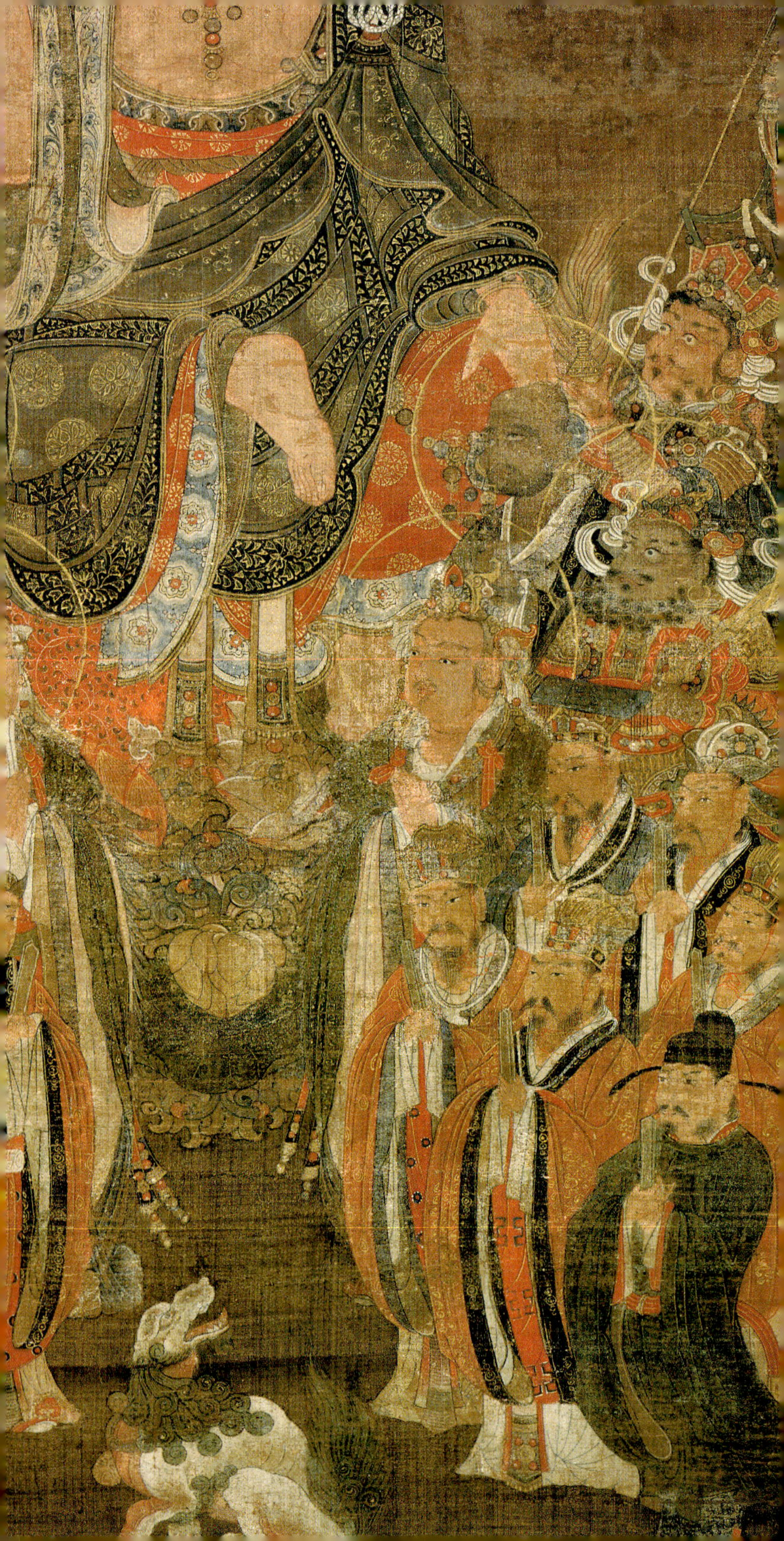

KOREA

In the West, Korean art lingered for a long time in the shadow of its neighbours, China and Japan. Only in recent decades has there been a serious effort to study the unique qualities of Korean art and culture. This belated appreciation has, unfortunately, meant that there is a painful gap in the collection of the Museum of East Asian Art. The Korean section of the collection consists of no more than a few dozen objects, certainly not an adequate reflection of the true place of Korean art in East Asia.

By far the most substantial group of objects in the Korean section of the collection is the ceramic bowls from the Chosŏn period (1392–1910), which at first captured the interest of Japanese masters of the tea ceremony and have been collected in Japan since the 16th century. Manufactured in Korea as ware for everyday use, their unaffected beauty matched the ideals of the tea ceremony. The basis for the Berlin collection of Korean ceramics, previously comprising well over one hundred objects, was laid through the early acquisitions of the museum, in the main from the estate of Japanese art dealer Hayashi Tadamasa (1853–1906). In 1915, ceramics from the Meyer-Große Bequest were added, some of which had originally been purchased from Hayashi. These new pieces significantly expanded the collection. This collection of Korean tea bowls could well have become the most significant collection of its kind outside of Japan today, had not 118 pieces ended up in the Hermitage Museum after the war.

With the opening of the newly designed galleries, the Museum of East Asian Art will for the first time in its history feature an area devoted entirely to Korean art. For the time being, the museum is dependent on loans to properly fill this particular exhibition area. Generous help has been provided by the Tōy ō Tōji Bijutsukan (Museum for Oriental Ceramics) in Osaka, by making a selection of exquisite objects from its famous collection of Korean ceramics available to the museum for a period of two years.

The importance of Korean art should not be understood solely as one of mediator between China and Japan, although this aspect does have an undisputed significance in the East Asian context. From the Neolithic period (ca. 6000–2000 BC) until the Three Kingdoms period (57 BC–AD 668) an autonomous culture evolved on the Korean peninsula, influenced to some degree by developments in north and central Asia and by local shamanism. Between the 4th and the 6th century, Buddhism spread from India across China and established a foothold in Korea, where it was the unchallenged official religion from the 6th century until the end of the Koryŏ period in 1392. Adopting influences from China, Korean artists and artisans gradually developed their own stylistic expression, which in turn influenced Japanese art. Buddhist images can be regarded as representative of this development. Korean ceramics, too, had a great influence on Japanese potters. The celadon ware of the Koryŏ period (935–1392) marks one of the highest achievements. These alone found their way into Western art collections, where their understated elegance was admired as being quintessentially Korean. When Confucianism was adopted as the official ideology by the Chosŏn period (1392–1910), another significant change occurred in art and culture, now defined by the needs and tastes of the cultural elite of the literati. The result was a secularization of themes as well as an increased focus on painting and calligraphy, which were essential elements in the classic ideal of the literati official. RS

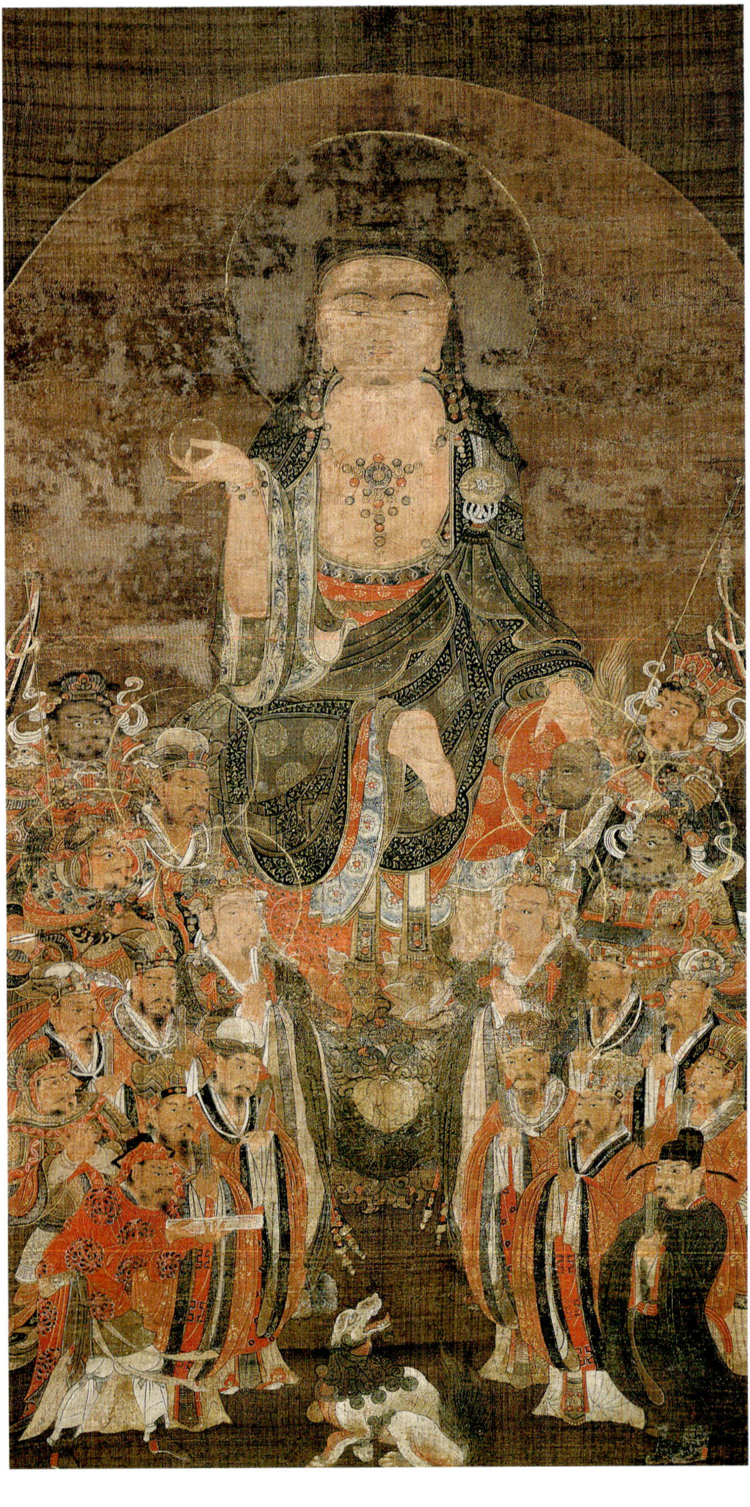

Unknown Master
Kṣitigarbha

Koryŏ period, 14th century
Hanging scroll
Ink and colour on silk
Height 109 cm, width 56.8 cm
Inv. No. 1966-14

Buddhism reached Korea from India via China between the 4th and 6th centuries, where it became the official religion during the Unified Silla period (668–935) and the Koryŏ period (935–1392). A large number of temples and sculptures of that era have been preserved, while Buddhist paintings of the Koryŏ period are rare, and those extant are mostly housed in Japanese collections.

The central figure in the scroll depicts the Bodhisattva Kṣitigarbha (Korean: Chijang). Bodhisattvas are benevolent deities in the Buddhist pantheon, whose compassion for human souls compels them to forgo their own ascendancy to Buddhahood. They regard it as their task to assist others in the path to enlightenment. Dominating the picture, Kṣitigarbha is seated on a lotus throne. He is clothed in an elaborately decorated robe, a monk's scarf, and precious jewellery. In his right hand he holds a *cintāmani*, a jewel with which he is able to grant wishes. Kṣitigarbha embodies compassion for all sentient beings and is the supreme master of the Ten Kings of Hell, who weigh good and evil deeds and pass judgment accordingly.

The companion figures are much smaller and also proportioned within the group in accordance with their position in the hierarchy. They are symmetrically arranged in two groups and integrated into the composition so as to emphasize the central position of Kṣitigarbha. Next to the Bodhisattva, beneath his left hand, stands the bearded monk Daoming; the figure on the opposite side in civil servant's robes is identified as the Ghost King Wudugui Wang. Both figures are closely related to Kṣitigarbha worship in Korea. Two other Bodhisattvas are placed on either side towards the middle. The group is flanked by guardian spirits: to the right the Guardian of the North with a pagoda and the Guardian of the East with a sword, to the left the Guardian of the West with a halberd and the Guardian of the South with two crossed arrows. These are followed by five Kings of Hell on each side. The Ruler of the Underworld can be seen at the bottom right margin, while a messenger holding a scroll rushes towards the group from the left, the only figure depicted in motion. The mythical beast seated in the middle depicts a lion, a manifestation of Mañjuśrī, the Bodhisattva of wisdom.

The delicate painting bears witness to the masterful skill of the unknown artist, who not only invested each portrait with individual traits but paid equal attention to the representation of material qualities and the ornamentation of the robes. Some comparable paintings in Japanese collections are dated to the 14th century. What these Korean paintings have in common are the broad, round faces of the frontally depicted figures, the elegant, fine-boned hands, the skilful rendering of transparent woven fabrics, the characteristic ornamentation, which is also found in Korean lacquerware of the same period, as well as the subtle colouring which favours red and green hues.

Wine jug

Koryŏ period, ca. 1200
Red-fired stoneware with *sanggam* decoration under grey-green celadon glaze
Height 23 cm, diameter 16.7 cm
Inv. No. 1962-1

The melon shape of this wine jug is typical of Korean stoneware. Decoration of the ten vertical sections alternates between stylized lotus and chrysanthemum vines. Foot and neck feature bands of leaf patterns. The lid – not originally intended for this jug – has twelve ribs and a knob shaped into a curlicue that is repeated on the handle, giving the jug a rather light-hearted character.

The *sanggam* inlay technique, developed as early as the 10th century and perfected in the 12th century, evolved independently in Korea. To create this type of decoration, derived from inlaid metalwork, the ceramic artist first carves the motifs into the unfired stoneware dried to a leather-hard consistency. The indentations thus created are filled with white or reddish brown slip, the latter turning black in the firing process. Excess slip is carefully removed before the vessel is covered in a celadon glaze. The transparent glaze, which usually crackles after firing, allows the design to be visible underneath. The balanced form and the graceful motifs had both been derived from the floral repertoire and reflect the Korean ideal of life in harmony with nature.

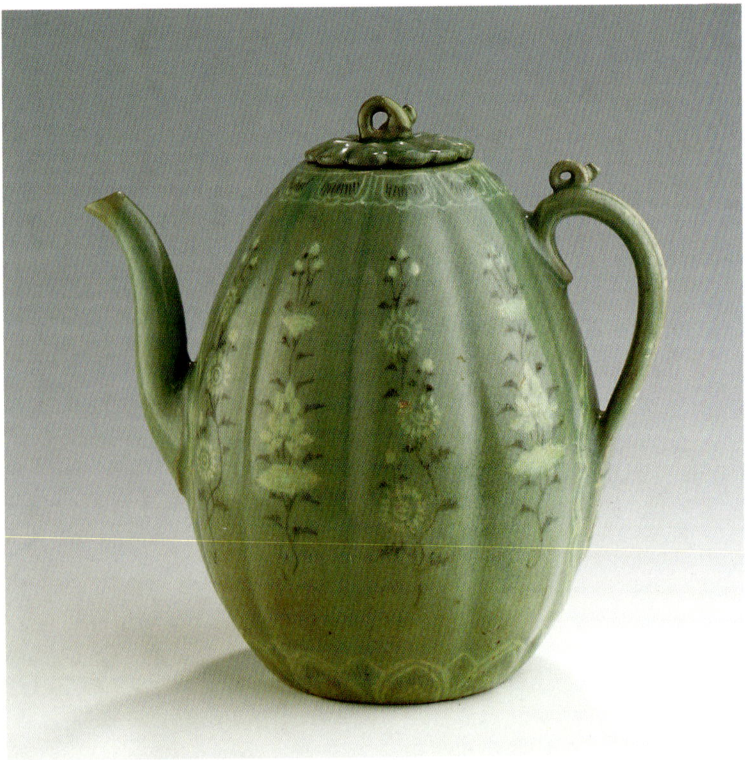

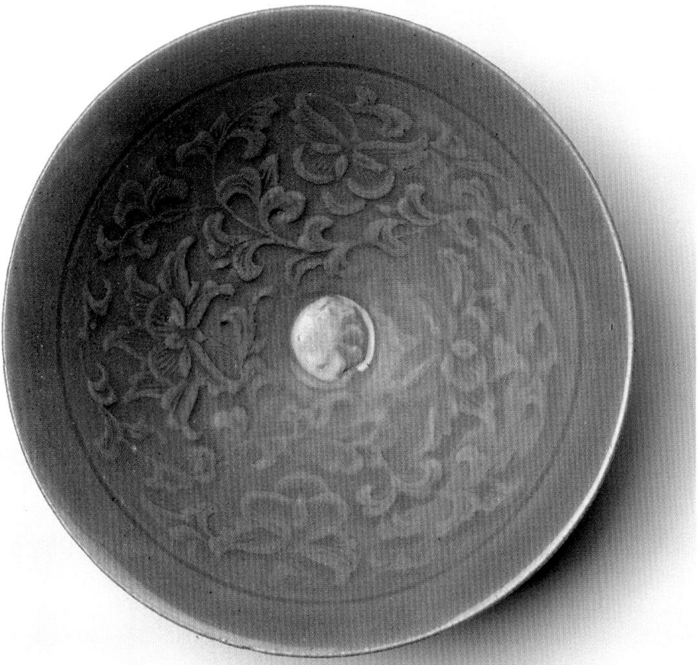

Bowl with relief decoration

Koryŏ period, 12th century
Porcelain with celadon glaze
Height 5 cm, diameter 16.1 cm
Inv. No. 1966-35

The fine, wide-mouthed bowl has a proportionately small foot ring, which contributes to the delicate appearance of the vessel. The impressed decoration covering the surface below the engraved ring depicts artfully scrolling peony vines, symbols of nobility and wealth. Leaves and flower petals are emphasized with fine interior detail. The celadon glaze appears darker in the indented areas than on the raised surfaces, creating an attractive sculptural effect. Celadon, as green-glazed ceramics are known in the West, were enormously popular in East Asia. In Korea, early production of such ware has been traced back to the 9th century. Manufacturing techniques and designs initially followed Chinese models. By the 12th century, however, Korean potters were creating unique vessels in which natural simplicity and refined elegance are beautifully combined, and which came to embody the best of Korean ceramics. Both in technical perfection and artistically accomplished form, these individual creations are among the highest achievements in East Asian ceramic arts.

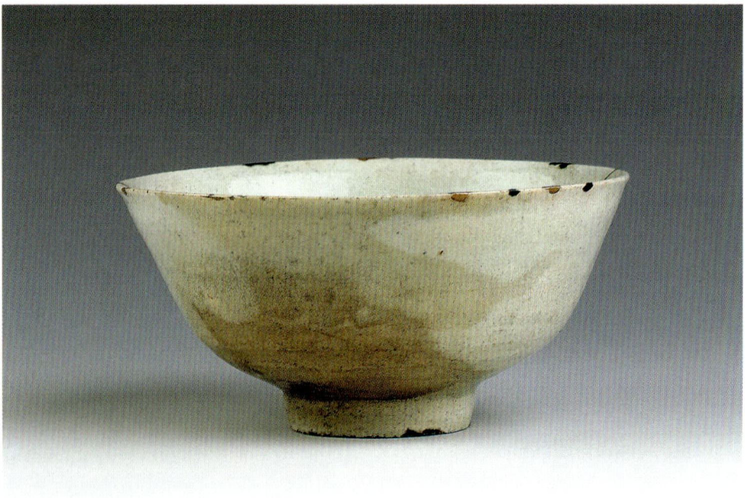

Bowl, *amamori-katade* type

Chosŏn period, 15th-16th century
Light stoneware with bluish cream-coloured glaze with pink and brown stains
Height 7.7 cm, diameter 15.8 cm
Inv. No. 427
Formerly Hayashi Tadamasa Collection

The wide bowl with a high foot has gently flared walls. It is covered in a bluish cream, finely crackled glaze with cloudy stains in a delicate pink and light and dark browns, creating the effect of an abstract watercolour. Five firing support marks are visible on the inside of the base. Old gold-lacquer repairs, executed in Japan, give the bowl an additional appeal. Bowls such as these were originally produced in Korea as ware for every-day use. They came to be appreciated as unique works of art and collector's items only from the early 16th century onwards by Japanese tea masters. The unpretentious charm of their simplicity, whose ingenuity often lies in accidental effects, corresponded to the aesthetics of the tea ceremony as practised by the great masters such as Sen no Rikyū(1522–1591). The division of tea bowls into different types was also undertaken in Japan, hence the Japanese names for these vessels. The term *amamori* used here refers to the spotty discoloration as a result of long use. This type of natural design was particularly appreciated in the tea ceremony. *Katade* designates the hard, porcellaneous body. Especially admired bowls were also given individual names. The value attributed to these bowls in Japan is also evident in the elaborate gold-lacquer repairs. Moreover, highly praised tea ware was stored in individual wooden boxes that reflected the vessel in shape and character. Thus this bowl is complemented by a brocade pouch and an inscribed wooden storage box.

Old Korean bowls, in greater numbers almost exclusively preserved in Japan only, exerted a strong influence on Japanese ceramics from the 16th century onwards.

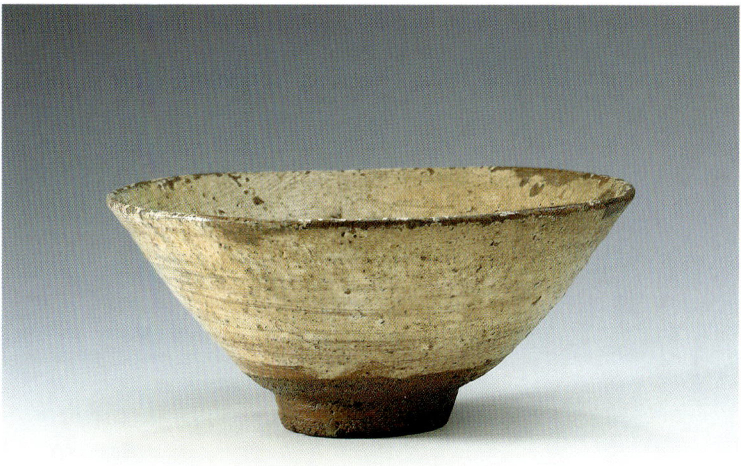

Bowl, *hakeme* type

Chosŏn period, 16th century
Red-brown body with transparent yellowish-beige glaze over white slip
Height 8.1 cm, diameter 18.5 cm
Inv. No. 438

The flared tea bowl with straightly ascending walls was covered in a layer of slip applied with a broad brush before being fired with a transparent yellowish beige glaze. Where the glaze formed droplets, a greenish shimmer is visible. The bowl has a number of aesthetic qualities that made it especially valuable in the eyes of tea masters: the rough body gives it a special tactile appeal and the red-brown tone is a pleasing contrast to the light glaze. The flowing traces of brushstrokes in the slip application and the carefree glazing, which leaves the foot unglazed and is allowed to gather into random droplets, invest the vessel with a rustic, spontaneous feeling. In addition, this tea bowl is accompanied by a brocade pouch and an inscribed wooden storage box.

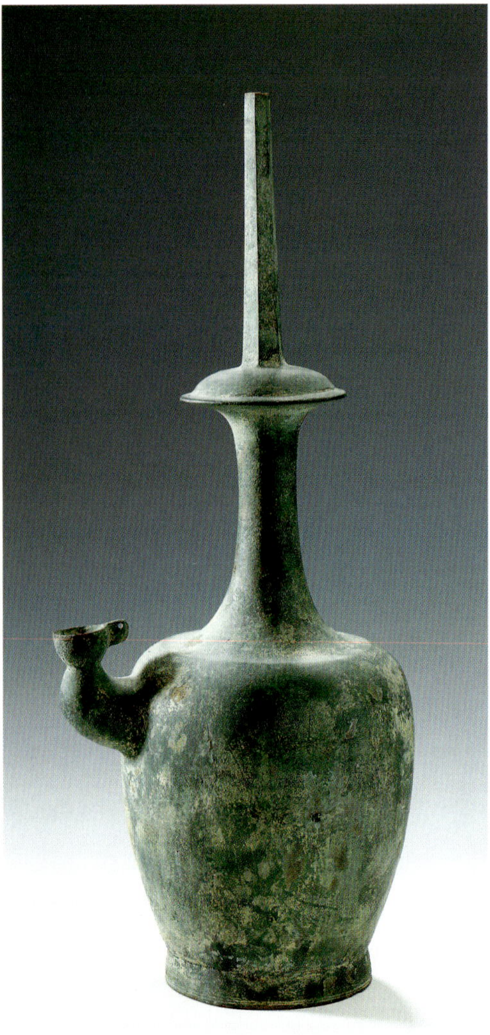

Chŏngbyŏng

Koryŏ period, 12th–13th century
Bronze
Height 38.5 cm, diameter 13.7 cm
Inv. No. 1968-19

Ritual vessels called *chŏngbyŏng* in Korean, meaning "bottle for pure water" (Sanskrit: kundikā), originated in India and were probably introduced to Korea with the spread of Buddhism during the Three Kingdoms period (ca. 57 BC–AD 668). Among the oldest types of Buddhist ritual vessels, they were used for the ceremonial sprinkling of water consecrated to Buddha. Since the 11th century the elegant form was also used for secular purposes, such as vessels for libations or as a vase.

From the gently sloped shoulder rises a tall neck that widens into a flat capsule from which the characteristic sexagonal spout emerges, which served to disperse the consecrated water. The stocky filling spout, attached to the side of the vessel, presents a strong contrast. Its original lid is missing. The bronze has a beautiful blue-green patina. *Chŏngbyŏng* were also produced in ceramic with celadon or white glaze.

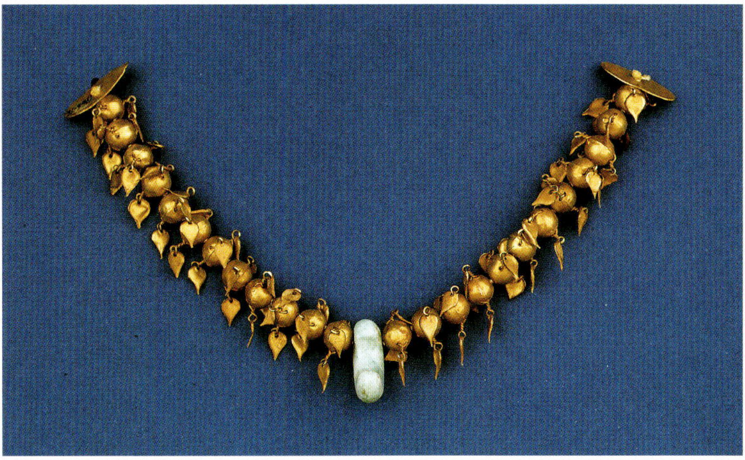

Gold necklace with jade pendant

Three Kingdoms period, Silla,
5th–6th century
Gold, gold wire, jade
Length 17 cm
Inv. No. 1966-16

The necklace, which may be part of a much larger chest adornment, consists of twenty-four hollow gold beads, to each of which are attached three small hanging gold plates; these tremble at any movement, being mounted on thin wires attached to the inside of each bead. The pendant is a C-shaped, matte, whitish-green piece of jade.

Shamanistic rituals played an important role in the pre-buddhist period of the Three Kingdoms. High-ranking nobles were buried with offerings of symbolic significance, intended to aid the deceased in his long journey to the underworld. Especially in the city of Kyŏngju and its environs, capital of Silla under the name of Kŭmsŏng, numerous tombs of rulers and nobles have been excavated, all with abundant gold jewellery offerings. The filigreed, elaborately worked jewellery is a testimony to the extraordinary craftsmanship of the goldsmiths of the kingdom, which was blessed with rich gold deposits.

Many of these gold crowns and necklaces bear C-shaped pendants, often made of jade, whose undoubted symbolic value has been variously interpreted: they may be regarded as depictions of predator teeth invested with magical powers, or as images of embryos and hence fertility symbols. Yet another thesis proposes that at least in some cases they could be seen as silkworms with whose intervention one hoped to implore the gods for success in silk production.

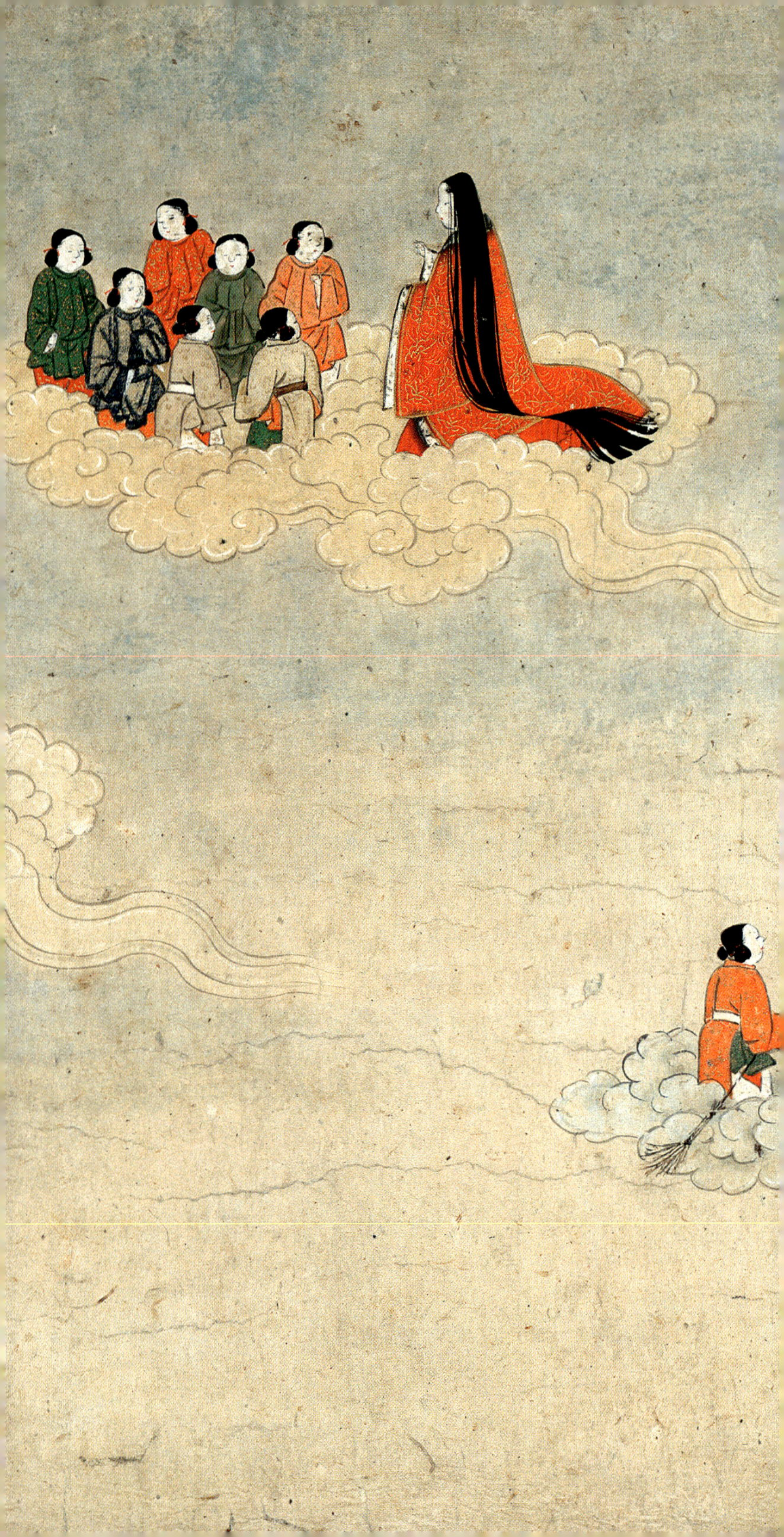

Japan

The pre-war collection at the Museum of East Asian Art, undoubtedly among the most important of its kind in Europe, was dominated by painting, tea ceramics – still fairly unknown in the West at the time (pp. 88–91) – and lacquerware (pp. 93–101): in other words, objects that meet the aesthetic criteria of a classic art collection. It is interesting to note that Japanese woodblock prints were not included in the early focus of the Museum collection as the artistic significance of these works was unappreciated at that time, both in Europe and in the country of origin, Japan. Buddhist and Shinto sculptures, too, received only moderate attention in the early development of the collection.

As is well known, World War II and its aftermath had devastating consequences for the collection of Japanese art. Fortunately, the three hundred objects that formed the basis for the post-war collection contained a number of outstanding Japanese paintings and tea ceramics. While the current holdings of Buddhist paintings, nearly all from the original collection, are rather modest in number, they are undeniably impressive in terms of artistic quality (pp. 80–85). The prized treasures of the museum, such as the narrative picture scroll *Amawakahikō sōshi emaki*, "The Tale of the Young Heavenly Prince Amawakahiko" (pp. 104–105), or the much-praised album of thirty-six poems (p.108), a joint creation of the prominent artists Hon'ami Kōetsu and Tawaraya Sōtatsu, are exhibits that have survived from the pre-war collection. Further, the collection of Japanese paintings contains eleven framed *nihonga*, which were donated to the museum by artists who participated in the exhibition "Works by Living Japanese Painters" in 1931 and which survived the turmoil of war (p. 114). A carefully planned acquisition policy made it possible to expand the painting collection in the post-war years despite limited means. Today, it contains representative works of all styles, including Muromachi-period ink painting (pp. 106–107), paintings from the Tosa school (p. 109), and Literati paintings (pp. 110–111).

In the arts and crafts area there was also a great need to catch up when the collection was being rebuilt. Among the most important new acquisitions are a set of five plates by the master ceramist Ogata Kenzan (p. 90) and the modern lacquer box "Forest Lake" (p. 101), created especially for the Berlin Museum by Taguchi Yoshikuni, an artist designated a National Living Treasure in Japan.

The Japan collection at the museum was tremendously enriched by the transfer of East Asian prints from the Art Library. In recognition of Japanese colour woodblock prints as works of art, the museum received some six thousand woodcuts and woodcut books of the highest quality (pp. 116–127) in 1967. Today, the Berlin collection of prints is internationally acclaimed, documented by several special exhibits in Japan and by the numerous requests for loans from renowned museums of East Asian art around the world.

The tradition of private patronage has recently been revived by Klaus F. Naumann's permanent loan to the Museum of part of his private collection. This varied collection comprises Chinese, Korean, and Japanese works of art, with the main focus on Japanese painting (p. 112) and lacquerware (pp. 94 to 95). In keeping with the importance of this collection, the Museum's new exhibition area will include a gallery devoted exclusively to these works. KT

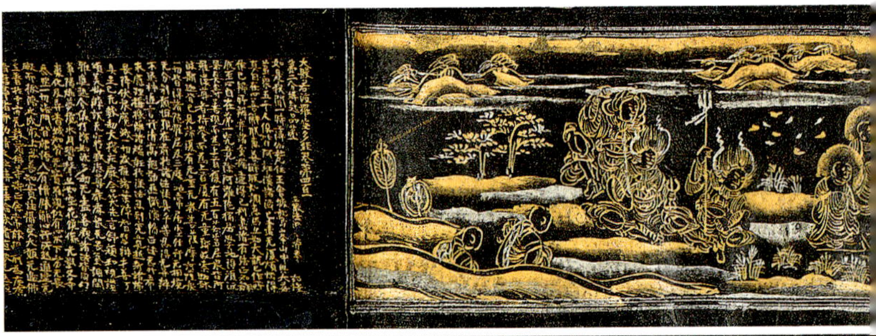

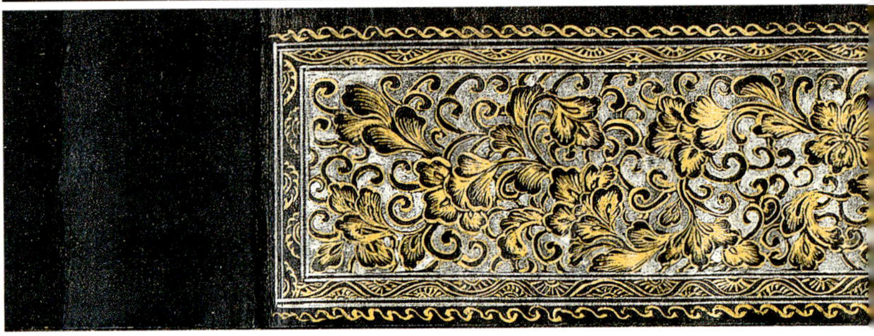

Sūtra of the Great Perfection of Wisdom

Late Heian period, 12th century
Fifty miniature handscrolls, painting and calligraphy in gold and silver on indigo-tinted paper
Each scroll 4.4 x approx. 200 cm
Inv. No. 214

Among the most sacred and most important texts of Mahayana Buddhism is the *Sūtra of the Great Perfection of Wisdom* (*Mahā-prajnāpāramitā-sūtra*; J: *Daihannyaharamitta-kyō*). It comprises 600 chapters, which the famous Chinese pilgrim monk Xuanzang (596–664) brought from his travels in India and translated into Chinese between 659 and 663.

These Buddhist teachings contain sermons which Buddha is said to have given to his disciples and lay followers over the course of sixteen meetings on the Vulture Peak in Magadha and at three other sites.

Since the 8th century, it was a popular practice among the aristocracy and clerics of Japan to write sūtra texts on lavishly decorated paper. Copying the sacred scripture was considered a religious observance, while at the same time thought to have a propitious effect. Sūtras were generally copied onto paper that had been dyed dark blue with indigo. The script and illustrations were executed in gold and silver.

The set in the Berlin Collection is said to have consisted originally of sixty miniature scrolls. However, ten scrolls were removed in 1784 due to insect damage. The remaining fifty scrolls each contain ten chapters. The cover sheet (*hyōshi*) is decorated with lavish, stylized flowering vines (*hosoge*). The cover sheet also bears a cartouche in which the number of each scroll and the corresponding title are inscribed.

On the first inside leaf, each scroll begins with a scenic depiction of Buddha's sermon to his disciples and lay followers. This scene is embedded into a stylized, generic landscape. This is followed by the individual chapters, each separated by a title page.

Several scrolls are kept in a black lacquer box, with mystical auspicious syllables in the Siddham alphabet on

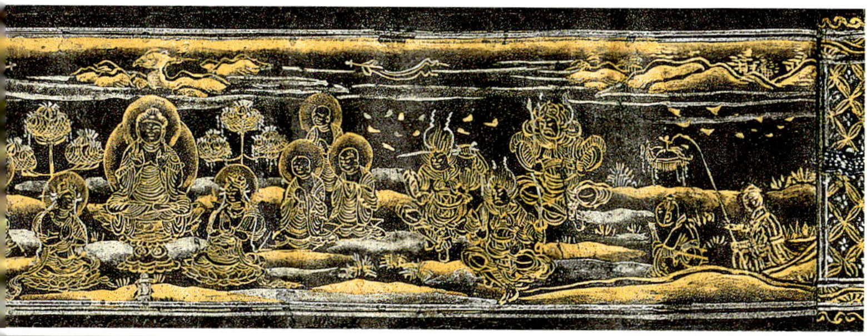

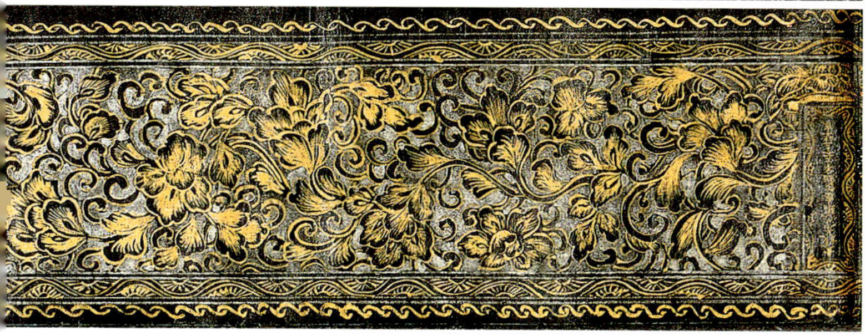

the red lacquered interior surface. Six such boxes, wrapped in brocade covers, fill the large lacquered storage container executed in the *negoro* technique. The container lid is inscribed with a Chinese poem.

An illustrated chronicle of Settsu province from 1792 mentions the sūtra set in the Berlin Collection, then in the possession of the Sumiyoshi Shrine, Osaka. According to the author of the chronicle, Akisato Ritō, the script and image are from the hand of Empress Kōmyō (701–760). However, the technical execution of the painting points to a work of the 12th century.

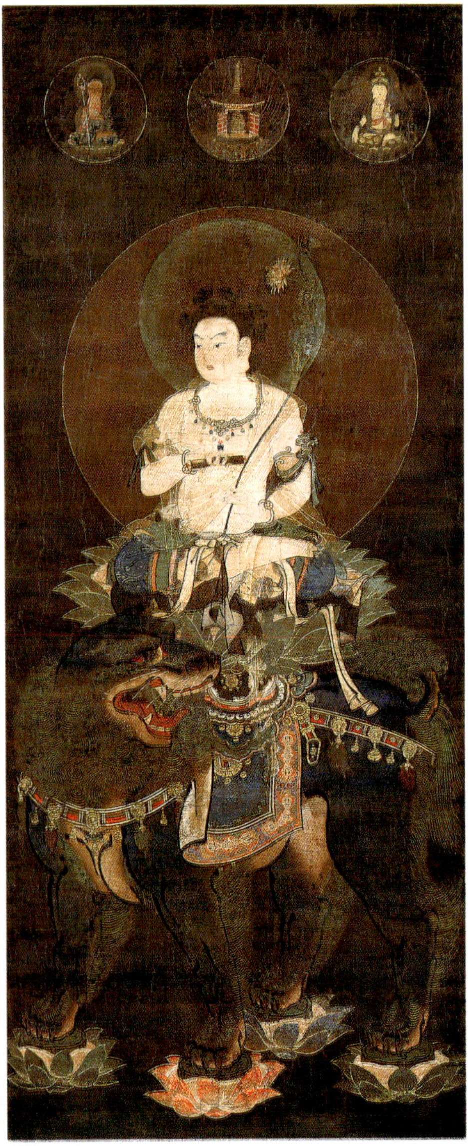

The youthful Monju Bosatsu, the Bodhisattva of metaphysical wisdom, is seated on a lotus throne and mounted on his companion beast, a blue lion. The fierce lion, who stands on four lotus flowers, is shown from the side, his head dramatically turned to the right. Monju Bosatsu appears serene, his face slightly turned to the left to give a three-quarter profile. In his left hand Monju carries a long-stemmed lotus flower; in his right, a sūtra scroll. His hair is tied into five knots, symbolizing the five Wisdom Buddhas of esoteric Buddhism, or rather, the five mystical syllables associated with them.

This representation differs from standard Monju images in the tradition of esoteric Buddhism through the presence of three small circles above the nimbus that surrounds the body. From right to left one can recognize: the eleven-headed Kannon Bosatsu, a Nyōrai figure (probably Shaka Nyōrai) in a pagoda, and Jizō Bosatsu. In this constellation the three figures represent the Buddhist manifestation of the Shintō deities of the Kasuga Shrine. Thus Monju can here be identified as the Buddhist manifestation of Kasuga Wakamiya.

This work is typical of the oeuvre of Buddhist master painters in the second half of the Kamakura period and is an outstanding example of the art of syncretistic Buddhism.

***Monju Bosatsu*, the Bodhisattva of Wisdom**

Late Kamakura period, late 13th to early 14th century
Hanging scroll, colour and gold on silk
105.6 x 44.8 cm
Inv. No. 3604

Jizō Bosatsu

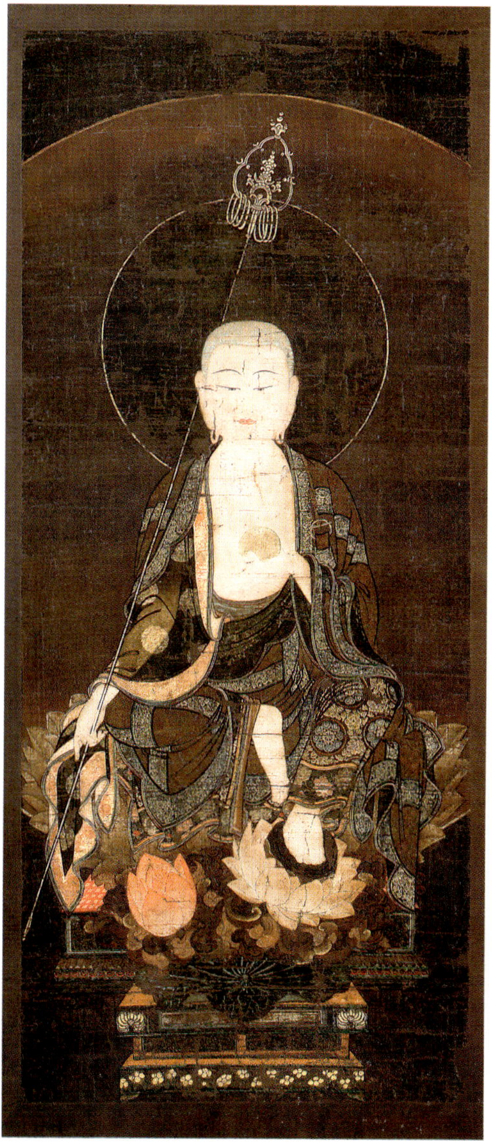

Late Kamakura period,
13th–14th century
Hanging scroll, colour and gold on silk
117 x 50.5 cm
Inv. No. 3570

Jizō Bosatsu, shown as a youthful monk, is seated in a casual pose, his right leg folded beneath him and the left rests on a lotus base. He is shown in a serene frontal view on a lotus throne with a two-tiered base. His attributes: the monk's robe, the auspicious jewel, and the staff typical of mendicant monks point to the early iconography of Jizō Bosatsu, popular in Japan since the beginning of the Kamakura period (1185–1333).

With the rise of Pure Land Buddhism in Japan in the 12th century, Jizō Bosatsu was increasingly recognized as one of the most important Buddhist deities. He was considered the only Bodhisattva (J: Bosatsu) to have remained in the physical world after the ascension of the historical Buddha Shakyamuni (J: Shaka Butsu) into Nirvana and also to be an embodiment of Miroku, the Buddha of the Future, who assists human souls on their voyage through the six levels of existence. Jizō Bosatsu continues to be popular in Japan as a guardian deity of children, of the weak and helpless, and of travellers.

The flower decoration on the two-tiered base and the treatment of the robe pattern with fine gold painting on a green and red ground are modelled on Song-dynasty Chinese paintings. The subtle facial expression and the delicate gold painting are typical of the religious painting of the late Kamakura period.

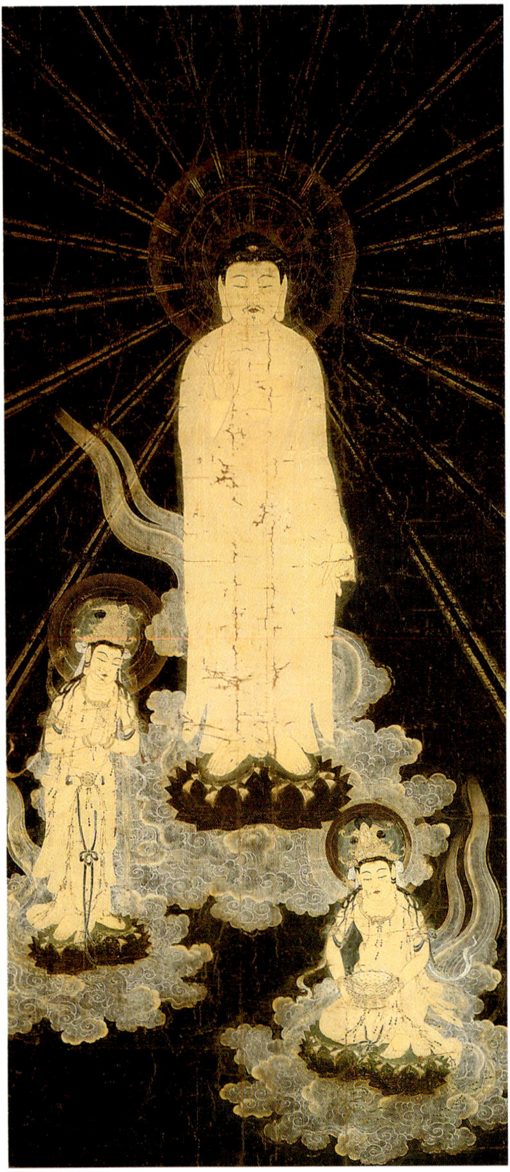

Descent of the Amida Triad

Kamakura period, 14th century
Hanging scroll, ink, colour, and gold on silk
152 x 69 cm
Inv. No. 215

Amida Buddha, the central figure, stands on two separate lotus platforms. Resting on stylized cloud bands, he is descending to welcome the souls of the deceased believers and to accompany them to the Western Paradise. He is flanked by Seishi Bosatsu on the left, bowing slightly and with folded hands, and Kannon Bosatsu on the right, kneeling and holding an open lotus blossom, ready to serve as the seat for the soul of the deceased.

In Japan, there are two standard compositions on this theme, known as *raigō-zu*. In the first, only the central figure of Amida Buddha is depicted in full frontal view; the second composition has a far more complex structure in which the central figure, shown in partial profile, is accompanied not only by Seishi and Kannon Bosatsu but also by a number of other Bodhisattvas. This scroll represents a blend of these two types. The frontal, statuesque depiction of Amida Buddha is typical of *raigō-zu* from the Kamakura period.

Kasuga Shrine Mandala

Nambokuchō to early Muromachi period, 14th–15th century
Hanging scroll, ink and colour on silk
101.2 x 37.3 cm
Inv. No. 1768

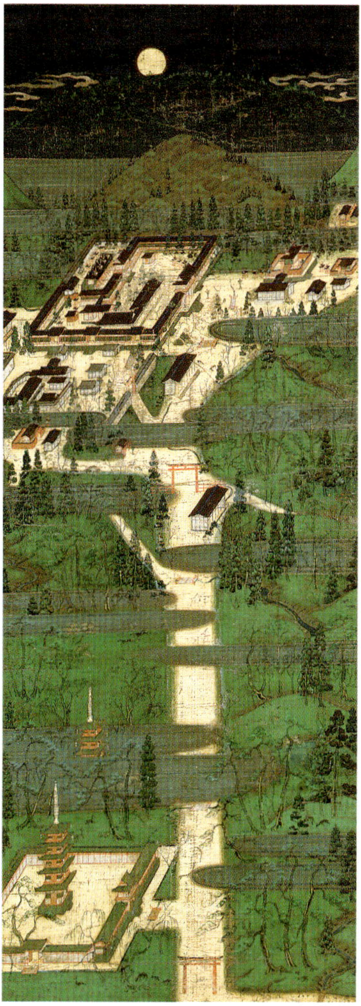

The Kasuga Shrine – one of the seven highest-ranking Shintō shrines in Japan – is located at the foot of the Mikasa and Kasuga mountains in Nara. The pilgrim route along the vertical axis of the image links the expansive shrine district in the upper third with the corresponding Buddhist temple Kōfuku in the foreground. The forests on either side are populated with stags, wild boars, and monkeys. Blue and green pigments, characteristic of the indigenous painting style, *yamatoe*, dominate the colouring of the scroll. The decorative effect of the image is further enhanced by the abundant use of gold, emphasizing above all the significance of the sacred districts and the pilgrim route.

According to syncretistic belief, the native Shintō deities are manifestations (*suijaku*) of Buddhist divinities, who represent their eternal form (*honji*). From the 12th century onwards, different types of cult images were introduced, illustrating the harmonious coexistence of these two religious traditions.

Rituals to honour Kasuga deities, originally revered as guardians of the powerful Fujiwara clan, are mostly depicted in two types of images: the deer mandala, *Kasuga shikamandara*, and the shrine mandala, *Kasuga miyamandara*. Depictions of the latter usually include Buddhist manifestations of the four Kasuga deities in the uppermost area of the scroll; this section is missing, however, in this example.

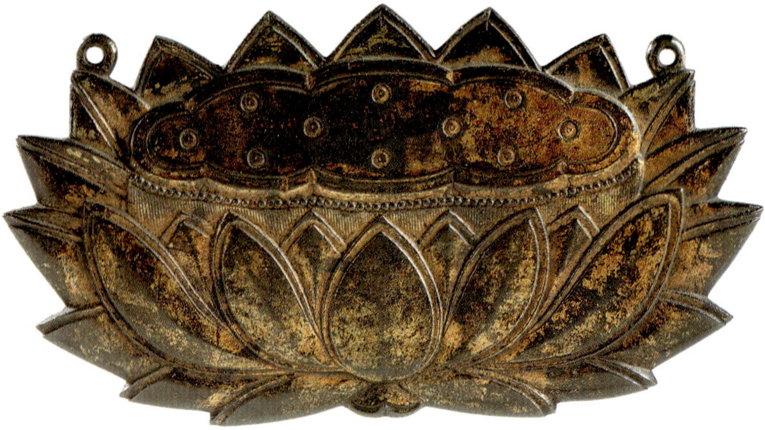

Ritual chime, *kei*

Late Kamakura period, 13th–14th century
Bronze with traces of gilt
8.9 x 16.8 cm
Inv. No. 1971-3

The chime is one of several ritual objects used in esoteric Buddhism.

During ceremonies the priest is seated in the temple hall in front of a low table on which water and incense burners and a variety of other objects are arranged following a specific pattern that symbolizes a mandala. The chime, suspended from a lacquered wooden frame, is positioned on the right. It is struck with a small wooden hammer. Initially imported from China, the chime was developed by Japanese craftsmen during the Heian period. The earliest chimes produced in Japan are of a simple geometric shape with a raised middle section, which serves as a resonating area. During the late Heian and the early Kamakura period, the surface decoration became increasingly elaborate and imaginative.

The classic model depicts the silhouette of a mountain, generally with a lotus blossom in relief shown from above or two facing peacocks in the middle.

This example is one of an extremely rare group of chimes cast in the shape of a lotus blossom. The resonating field is an eight-lobed seed pod with the seeds indicated by small engraved circles. Each flower petal is defined through two parallel contour lines, which produce a sculptural effect.

One of the most symbolic plants in Buddhism, the lotus serves as a metaphor for enlightenment and a symbol of purity. In addition, the seed pod has auspicious significance.

Zao Gongen

Heian period (second half of 12th century)
Bronze
Height 23.5 cm
Inv. No. 1979-4

The originally nameless Shintō deity of the Kinpu mountain near Yoshino, in the vicinity of Nara, was honoured in the Zao Hall of the mountain temple as a guardian deity against all evil. The addition of "Gongen" to his name indicates that this local deity is to be understood as a manifestation of a Buddhist deity. Zao is generally revered as the Shintō manifestation of Miroku Butsu (*Maitreya Buddha*), the Buddha of the Future. Especially in the 11th century, when civil war and clan disputes reinforced the belief in Buddha's prophecy of the end of the world, the Zao cult gained in popularity in Japan. Zao sculptures were buried as guardian figures together with sacred scripts that were to be saved from the impending end of the world.

Reflecting this guardian function, Zao figures are depicted in a warrior stance. Characteristics include a muscular physique and a fierce facial expression with thick eyebrows and a pronounced ridge above the nose, as well as hair that rises from the head in the form of flames, a menacing glance, and bared fangs. The sculptural execution is enhanced through the great dynamic energy of the figure: while the right foot is raised in readiness to stamp out evil, the left is firmly planted on a rock. Zao Gongen's right arm is raised high, his hand clenched in a fist, and the left arm is pressed against his body in the so-called "sword-holding pose."

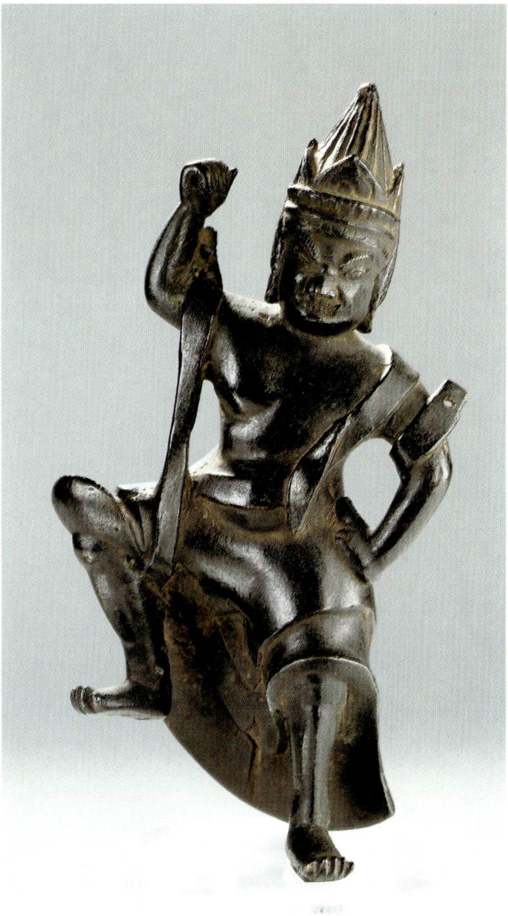

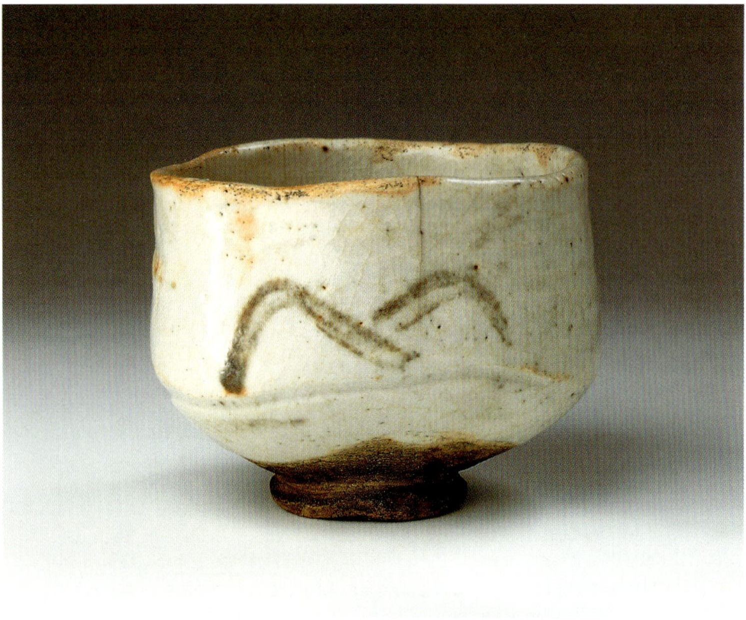

Tea bowl, *chawan*

Ōgaya, Mino, *e-Shino* type ware
Momoyama period, last quarter of 16th century
Sand-coloured, reddish discoloured body, underglaze in iron-oxide red and brown
Grey-white crackled feldspathic glaze
Height 10.1 cm, diameter 14 cm
Inv. No. 23

This tea bowl is considered an exquisite example of *e-Shino* type ware ("painted" Shino) from Ōgaya in Mino province (modern Gifu prefecture). The irregularly shaped bowl on a sturdy foot displays the sparse decoration typical of Shino ware beneath a thick yet transparent glaze. An engraved line describes a circle around the entire bowl at hip height. This is referred to in Japan as a "mountain path," *yamamichi*. Immediately above this line, two mountain silhouettes and a fence pattern are sketched in. A similarly sketchy linear decoration graces the inside of the bowl. A firing crack, filled with a thin layer of gold lacquer, provides an additional accent, as does the very delicate *hi-iro* (fire colour) of the glaze along the rim, which is especially appreciated by masters of the tea ceremony.

In shape and decoration, this *chawan* is a fine example of the Shino tea bowls fired in Ōgaya. In the 15th century the production of such glazed ceramics shifted from the traditional Seto kilns in Owari to Mino in the west, where experiments were undertaken with new glazes, decoration, and shapes. Shino ceramics were fired from the mid-16th century onwards and were manufactured almost exclusively for the tea ceremony. Characteristics include a coarse-grained, yellowish body and an opaque white glaze brought to a gentle glow from use. These *e-Shino* wares are among the earliest Japanese ceramics with underglaze painting.

Water jar, *mizusashi*

Edo period, 17th century
Echizen or Tokoname
Heavy, reddish-grey stoneware, yellowish glaze along the edge and on the inside
Black lacquered wooden lid
Height 13.4 cm,
max. diameter 23.5 cm
Inv. No. 1190

The character painted on the bottom of this heavy, coarse water jar, *iwao* (rock), expresses the potter's intent to create a piece that gives the impression of having been hewn from rock. Two of the opposite walls of the *mizusashi* display a zigzag edge, creating a tension in the contour of a form that is otherwise simple and without artifice. The lacquered lid that is common for such water jars fits precisely. This type of deliberate design is characteristic of tea ceramics of the Edo period created under the influence of the tea ceremony master Kobori Enshū (1579– 1647), whose elegant style stands in contrast to the simplicity of Sen no Rikyū's (1522–1591) tea ceremony.

The reddish-grey body of the *mizusashi* in the Berlin Collection points to an origin in Echizen or Tokoname (modern Aichi prefecture). Unglazed, fairly large ceramics for everyday use were manufactured in the region as early as the medieval period. In the Momoyama period, and again increasingly during the second half of the Edo period, ceramics for the tea ceremony were also produced in Tokoname. In this ware too the focus lay in producing unglazed, extremely well-fired (*yakishime*) pieces, which were made stone hard and impermeable as a result of the firing process. This *mizusashi* is a good example of such ware. The *mizusashi* is one of the most important vessel types in the tea ceremony, as it holds the water used for tea preparation.

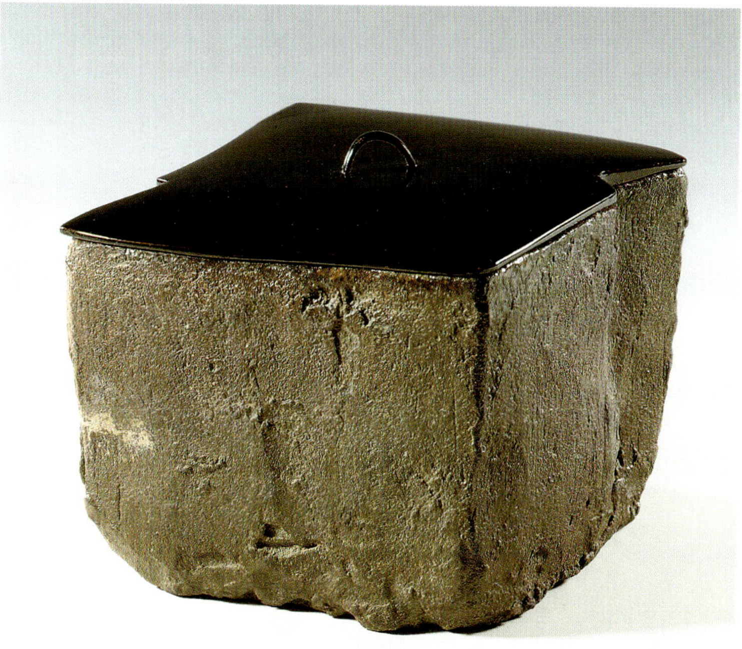

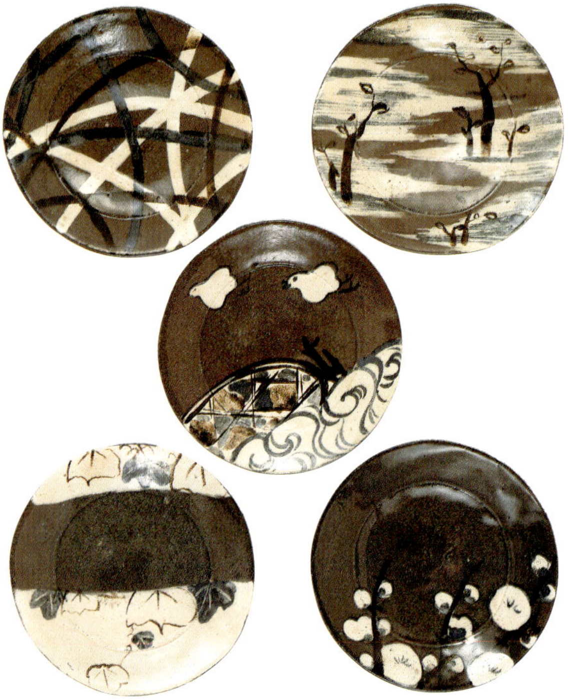

Set of five small plates

Ogata Kenzan (1663–1743)
1712–1731
Slip and underglaze painting with transparent glaze
Signature (on the base of each plate): *Kenzan*
Height 0.6–1 cm,
diameter approx. 12.6 cm
Inv. No. 1972-13 a-e

The calligrapher and potter Ogata Kenzan, like his brother Ogata Kōrin (1658–1716), was a member of the *Rinpa* school (17th–19th century) which practised a Japanese style of painting that was first developed by Tawaraya Sōtatsu (active ca. 1600–1640). This style is characterized by a decorative manner in which stylized motifs lend a rhythmic structure to the surface, as in these examples. Each of the five plates has a different motif: grasses, flowering plum, ivy, plovers above waves and a snowy landscape.

The decorative images on the hand-formed plates are applied with slip and underglaze painting. The warm earth tones of the body and of the painting are combined with a matte blue and covered in a transparent glaze. Kenzan's Narutaki kiln was near the Ōmuro kiln of the famous ceramic artist Nonomura Ninsei (ca. 1627–1695) in Kyoto. From him, Kenzan inherited a valuable secret manuscript, the *Tōhō densho*. In matters of decoration, Kenzan collaborated closely with his brother, Kōrin.

Four similar sets of five plates are preserved in three Japanese collections, among them the collection of the Nezu Museum in Tokyo. The calligraphic signature on the base indicates that these plates were made at the Chojiya-chō workshop in Kyoto. Numerous works signed by Kenzan were produced at this site between 1712 and 1731.

Bowl in the shape of a boat

Edo period, late 17th–early 18th century
Kyōyaki, Kyoto
Under- and overglaze painting, beige crackled glaze, heavy light-yellowish body
Height 7.6–10.4 cm, width 18.2 cm, length 29.5 cm
Inv. No. 157-1999
Klaus F. Naumann Collection

The boat-shaped oval bowl with a straight base opens into a wide, flaring wall at the hip and tapers to a point at either end. It is covered with an overall floral vine pattern. The underglaze decoration is executed in blue and black on the inside; the rim is also painted in black underglaze.

The outside surface is decorated with flowering peonies and vines executed in slightly raised overglaze painting of blue, green, and gold. The bottom is unglazed. The bowl is a fine example of early Kyoto ware (Kyōyaki), produced from the mid-17th century onwards, whose formal and painterly characteristics are distinctly different from the spare colouring of *raku* ware, also produced in Kyoto. The colourful ceramic ware, decorated with motifs borrowed from scroll paintings, was produced in numerous workshops and kilns in and around the imperial city of Kyoto. These multicoloured tea ceramics with often unusual shapes were compatible with the trend towards a more luxurious style in the tea ceremony as it was performed in aristocratic homes. Next to Ogata Kenzan (1663–1695), Nonomura Ninsei (ca. 1627–1695) was the leading ceramic artist working in the new style. Traditionally, Ninsei is associated with the foundation of the Mizoro kiln in Awataguchi near Kyoto, to whose products this bowl is closely related. The so-called *ko-kiyomizu* ware was produced in the workshops around the Kiyomizu temple in Kyoto, to which this piece is also related.

The box for the bowl bears an inscription that attributes the bowl to *ko-kiyomizu* ware and to Ninsei.

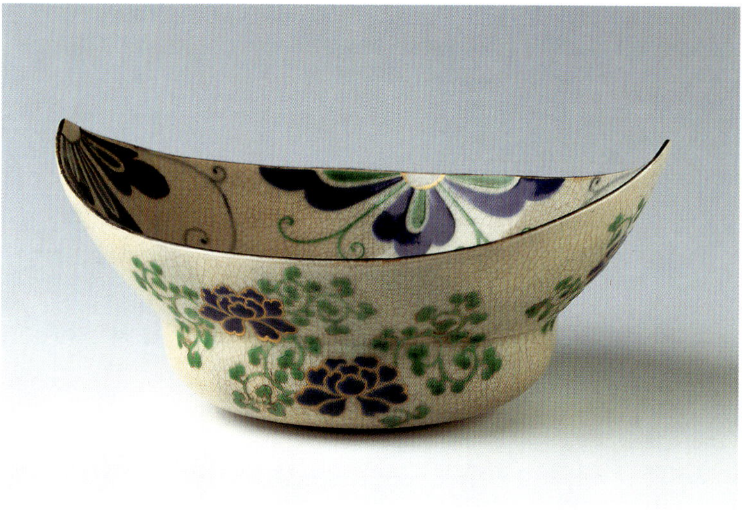

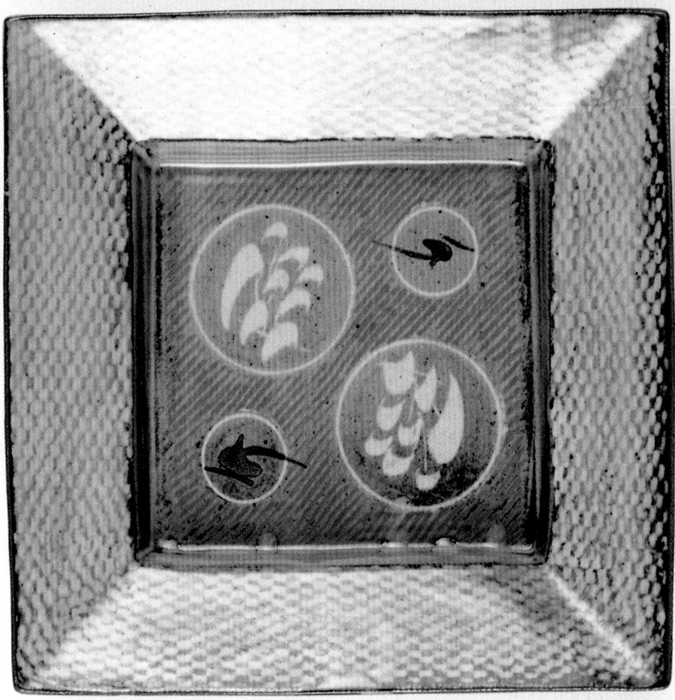

Square plate

Shimaoka Tatsuzō (born 1919)
Square plate with Jōmon pattern, slip and underglaze painting with semi-transparent Mashiko glaze on coarse, reddish brown body
Signature: *Tatsuzō*; red seal: *Tatsuzō*
Height 5.9 cm, width 27.2 cm, length 27.5 cm
Inv. No. 1990-14

The decorative elements used on this earthenware plate are typical of Shimaoka Tatsuzō's work. Gracefully curving grasses made of slip inlaid into the clay using the *zōgan* technique animate the geometrically arranged medallions defined by clear lines. The underglaze floral design, skilfully executed in iron oxide, provides additional accents. Shimaoka achieved the structure of the light-blue background by combining the *jōmon* technique in which a rope is pressed into the leather-hard clay and the Korean *mishima* technique in which slip is poured into an incised design. The balanced decorative elements are covered in a semi-transparent glaze. Shimaoka Tatsuzō's work is influenced by the *Mingei-kyōkai* (Folk Art Movement), which inspired him to study the Japanese ceramics of the Jōmon period (until ca. 250 BC) and the popular Korean ceramics of the Chosŏn dynasty (1392–1910). He studied with Hamada Shōji (1894–1978) in Mashiko. Like his master, Tatsuzō perpetuates the ideals of the *Mingei* movement founded by Yanagi Sōetsu (1889–1961) in the late 1920s, in which traditional techniques were revived. Shimaoka's oeuvre is defined especially by a Shintō reverence for nature and the concomitant preference for natural materials and simple, practical designs. While the early *Mingei* movement promoted a communal manufacturing process involving all members of a workshop, and therefore – by logical extension – pieces were not signed, Shimaoka, like his teacher Hamada, is known as an individual ceramic artist and much admired in Japan as a master of ceramics in the *Mingei* style.

Saddle, *kura*

Momoyama period, dated 1594
Black, red, and gold lacquer, glass on wood core, *hira-* and *takamakie*, *kirigane* on *nashiji*
Height 25.7 cm, width 39 cm, length 36 cm
Inscription: *Bunroku san nen hachi gatsu hi* and *Kakihan*
Inv. No. 4163

On a "pearskin ground", (*nashiji*), covered in gold lacquer, an image of a dragon emerging from ocean waves animates each pommel. The bodies of the dragons are "relief sprinkled pictures," *takamakie*, in gold. Bright red, flame-like tails around the legs of the dragons provide an attractive accent. They are realized as "flat sprinkled pictures," *hiramakie*, as are the animal claws in silver. The crests of the stylized waves stand out in black lacquer on the gold *nashiji* ground. Rectangular gold appliqué, *kirigane*, at the curves of the clouds produces additional light effects. The interior of the dragons' ears and the tongues are painted in red lacquer. The realistic execution of the eyes is worth noting: beneath convex glass lenses, the black pupils are painted onto a white ground. All other external surfaces are covered in gold with *nashiji* without further ornamentation. The underside of the harness is partially covered in fabric. This type of saddle is called *yamato-gura* or *wagura* (Japanese-style saddle) in difference to the earlier *karakura* type (Chinese-style saddle). While *karakura* saddles were used exclusively on ceremonial occasions, saddles of this type were employed in battle.

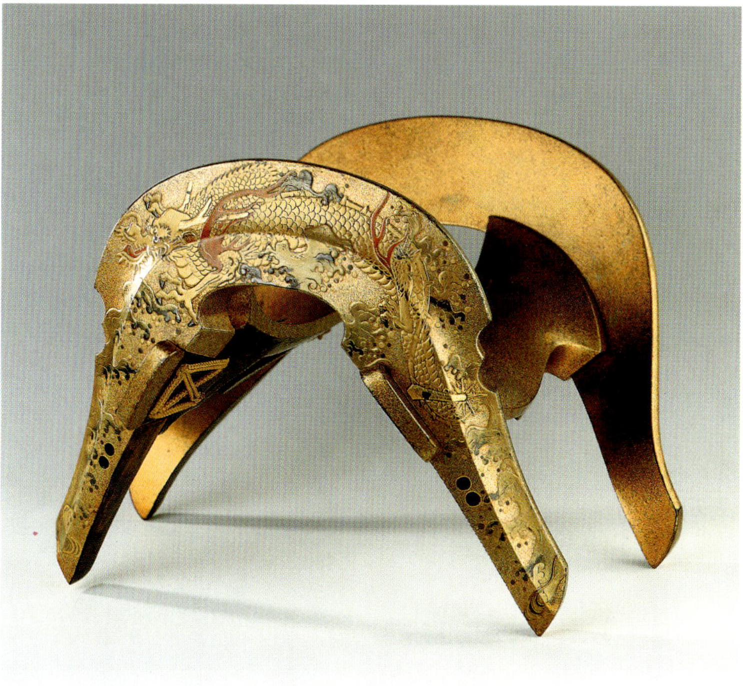

Drum body, *kotsuzumi*

Edo period, 17th century
Black, brown, gold, and silver lacquer on wood core, *hira-* and *takamakie*, *tsukegaki*, *harigaki* on *nashiji*
Length 25 cm, diameter 10 cm
Signatures (in drum body):
Kogosuke no Rō and *Seiju* (?) with *Kakihan* (written seal)
Inv. No. Dlg. 182-1999
Klaus F. Naumann Collection

The body of the drum is carved from a single piece of wood and shaped like an hourglass. Originally, lacquered horsehide was stretched across the top and bottom, held in place by rings larger in diameter than the openings and cross-braced with cords. In the Nara period (710–794) drums were introduced from the mainland that were larger and played with wooden drumsticks. This hand drum was held on the left shoulder with the left hand and played with the right hand; the drummer modulated the pitch by squeezing the cords with his left hand. *Tsuzumi* were the most important musical instruments in traditional Nō and Kabuki theatre. While the larger model (*ōtsuzumi*) produces a sharper sound and is accompanied by the drummer singing while he strikes his drum, the smaller model illustrated here (*kotsuzumi*) produces softer tones. These hand drums were elaborately decorated in *makie* techniques during the 16th and 17th centuries. The earliest pieces with gold-lacquer decoration date from the 14th century. The detailed artistic treatment of the body of the drums is a reflection of the supreme importance of the Nō theatre among the nobility. The Shogun Toyotomi Hideyoshi (1536 to 1598) performed in person during Nō theatre performances before the emperor. The design on the drum body is varied and often original, since no definitive motif tradition developed for *tsuzumi*. Plant motifs in the style of *Kodai-ji* lacquerware typical of the Momoyama period are common. In painted and sprinkled relief gold and lacquer decoration this drum depicts cloud ribbons between which the Wind god, *fujin*, bearing his wind-filled sack and the Thunder god, *raijin*, carrying his bow and arrow are shown in dynamic interaction. Both deities are represented alternately from the front- and backside and the design is applied in a manner that it can be read even upside down. The dramatic effect of the expressively drawn gestures and mimicry of *fujin-raijin* is enhanced yet further with details, such as musculature and eyes, engraved with a fine needle, *harigaki*. The hair of the two deities is worked in raised lines,

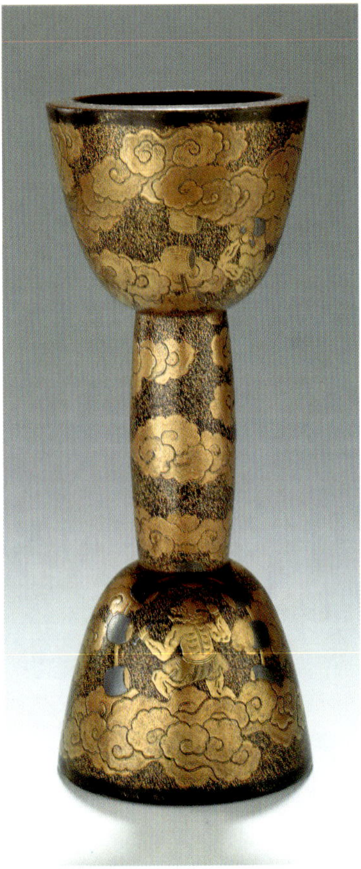

tsukegaki. Pictorial precedents for this dynamic play of Gods are found in the early-Edo-period paintings of the *Rinpa* school. Thus Tawaraya Sōtatsu (active 1600–1640) created his famous pair of screens – now housed in the Kennin-ji temple in Kyoto – on the same theme in the first third of the 17th century. A *ōtsuzumi* type drum with mother-of-pearl inlay, produced during the Muromachi period in the 16th century and housed in the Miho Museum, also features a continuous thunder-lightning motif between clouds, albeit without the figurative representation of the gods of wind and thunder. The drum in the Berlin Collection bears two signatures on the inside and a written seal, *kakihan*, in gold lacquer, which cannot be identified.

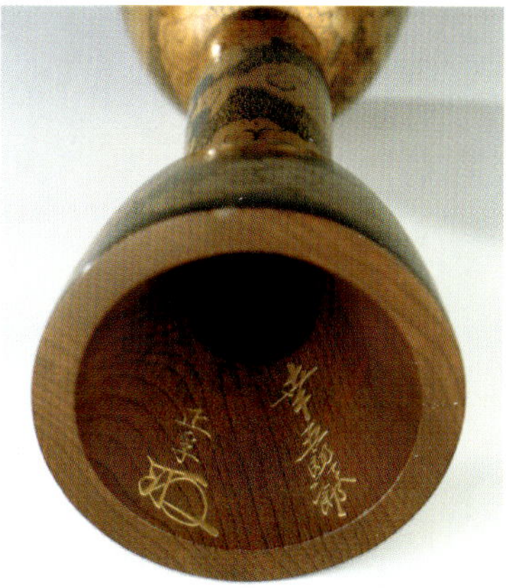

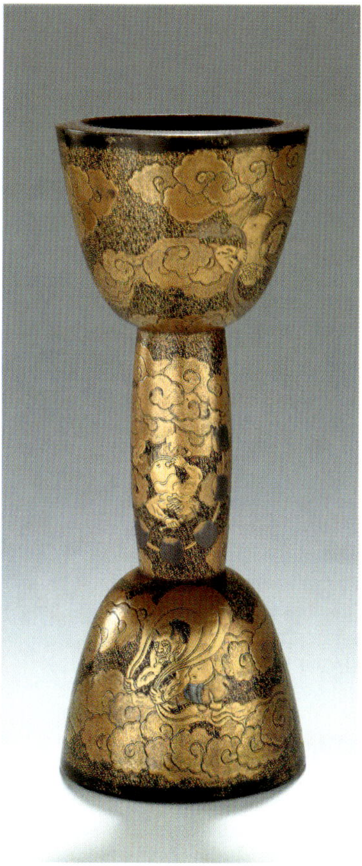

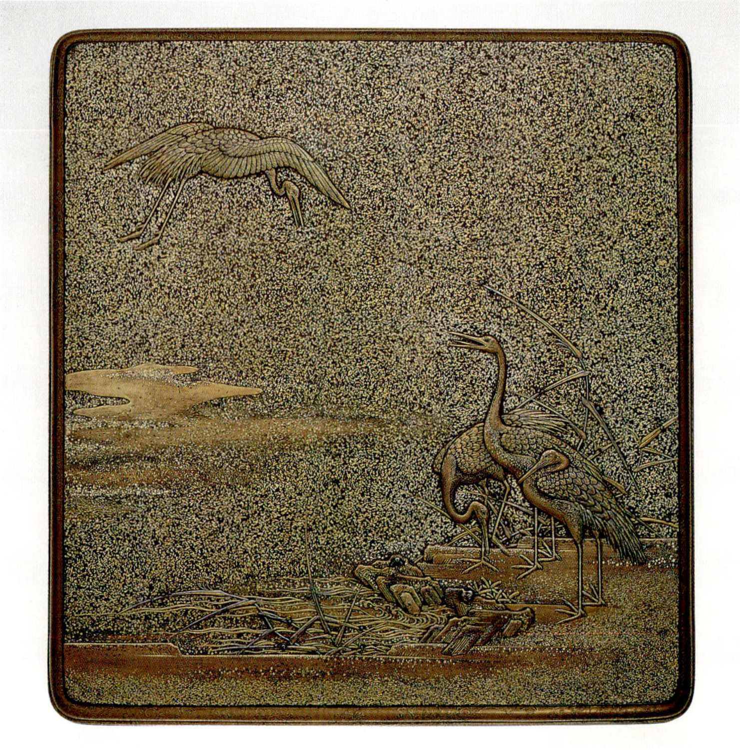

Writing box, *suzuribako*

Edo period, 17th century
Black, gold, silver lacquer and zinc on wood core (cypress), *hira-* and *takamakie*, *togidashi*, *kirigane*, *harigaki*, and silver appliqué on *nashiji*
Height 4.7 cm, width 23.3 cm, length 24.1 cm
Inv. No. 1810

The nearly square writing box with rounded corners and a flat lid points in its traditional form to earlier models from the 15th and 16th centuries. The box contains narrow compartments for brushes and paper knives on the right and left, flanking the central board with a surface for the inkstone, *suzuri*, and the opening above it for the water dropper, *mizuire*. The original utensils have not been preserved. The entire surface of the black lacquered writing box is sprinkled with fine gold particles, *nashiji*. The edges of the lid and bottom of the box and of the inner compartments are bordered in zinc. The design in gold and silver lacquer is executed in varying degrees of relief (*hira-* and *takamakie*). On the lid are three cranes on a reedy, rock-bordered riverbank, with a fourth crane flying towards them. Silver dewdrops and a ribbon of clouds that projects into the centre of the image convey an early morning atmosphere. The cranes, a symbol of longevity in East Asian art, are depicted in different attitudes. To enhance the plastic effect of the cranes' bodies worked in *takamakie* relief, fine lines, *harigaki*, are used to create a precise rendering of the plumage, heightening the realistic effect. The scene on the top of the lid is framed by a continuous band of stylized vine motifs, *karakusa*, in gold-lacquer painting.

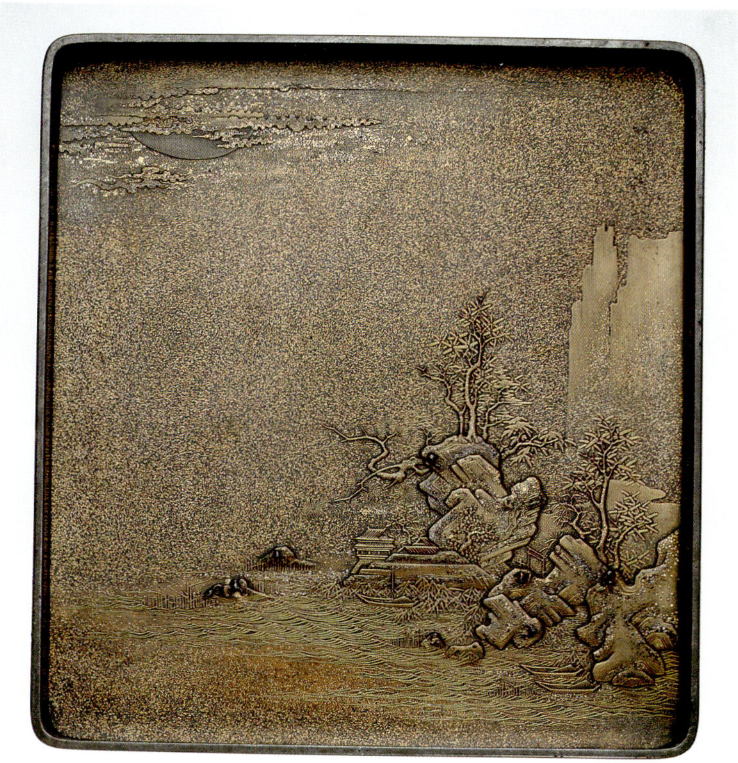

The inside of the lid bears the image of a Shintō shrine with a *torii* gate in a lonely river landscape. At the shore is a boat among the dense growth of reeds. A windswept pine on a rock and high mountain peaks in the distance are bathed in the light of a cloud-obscured moon. This type of landscape image, developed in Muromachi-period ink paintings, is continued on the compartments inside the box. A moonlit mountain or river landscape usually depicts a specific region familiar from the classic poetry collections. In the case of this *suzuribako*, the image may be drawn from the famous Sumiyoshi theme, whose iconography dates to the Muromachi period. Minamoto Yorimasa's (1105–1180) poem reads in part:

Gazing between the pines of the
Sumi River
Above the mountains of Awaji Island
I see the moon sinking.

The stylistic execution of the vine motifs and the relatively coarse gold powder of the *nashiji* ground date the piece to the first half of the Edo period.

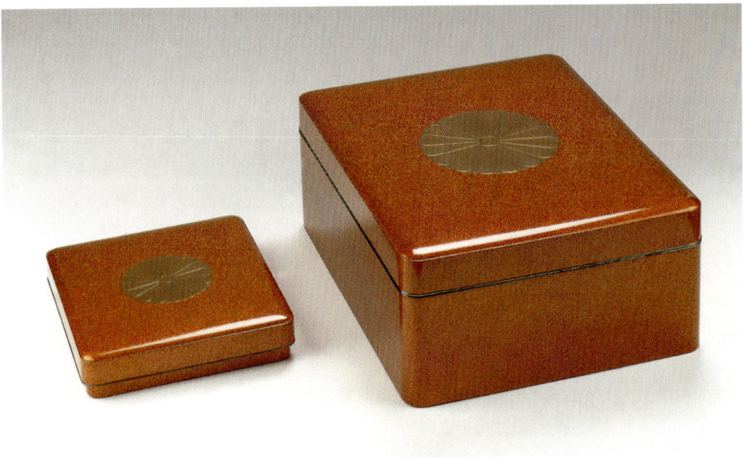

Writing box, *suzuribako* and paper box, *ryōshibako*

Meiji period, ca. 1900
Black, gold and silver lacquer on wood core, *togidashi*, *hira-* and *taka-makie*, *okibirame*, *harigaki* and *tsukegaki* on *nashiji*
Height 4.5 cm, width 22.3 cm, length 24.4 cm and
Height 16 cm, width 32.7 cm, length 41.3 cm
Inv. Nos. 1963-5/1963-6
Formerly E.H. Bälz Collection, Berlin

The writing box with its flat lid is nearly square. The four corners are rounded, and the edges of the lid are bevelled. The lid is almost imperceptibly convex and slightly larger than the box itself. The edges of the box and of the lid are encased in silver. The formal design of the writing box is based on classic models from the 15th and 16th centuries. The interior is completely preserved: the middle board holds the inkstone, *suzuri*, and the water dropper, *mizuire*, in the shape of a crane flying in front of clouds. The compartments to the left and right contain two brushes and an ink container as well as paper knives and an awl for punching holes in paper. The metal fittings on the last three pieces are decorated with cherry blossoms and maple leaves. The support struts in the compartments are carved to hold the writing utensils in a firm grip.

The lid is embellished with a stylized sixteen-petal chrysanthemum, the imperial emblem, in gold lacquer on a dense reddish "pearskin ground," *nashiji*. The inside lid shows a design with a partial view of the

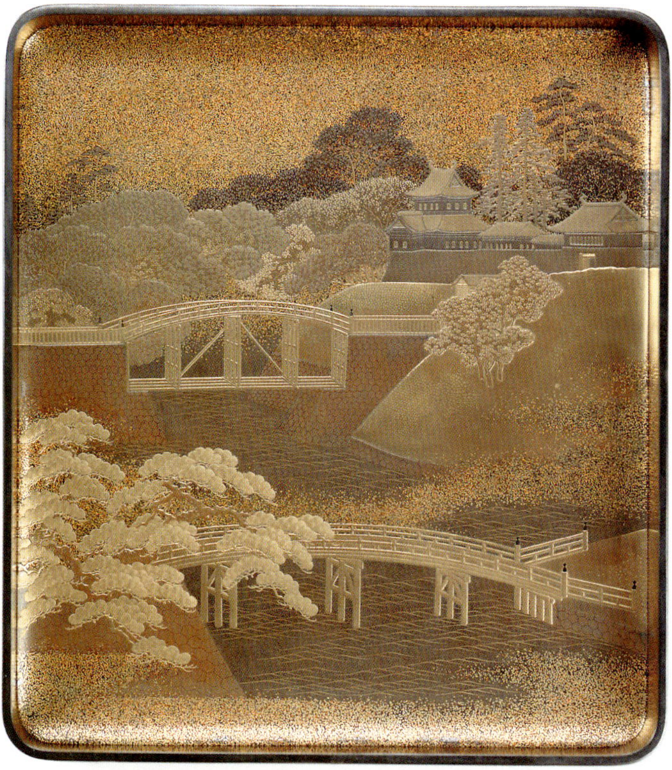

Imperial Palace in Tokyo with wall, moat, two bridges, and trees, all on a densely strewn yellowish *nashiji*.

As with the landscape design on the matching paper box (the larger box), the depiction of the Imperial Palace combines extreme care in the rendering of detail in various gold hues, silver, and black lacquer with a rich interplay of the classic gold-lacquer techniques of *nashiji*, *togidashi-makie* ("polished sprinkled picture"), *hira-* and *takamakie* ("flat and relief sprinkled picture"), *okibirame* (inlaid rectangular gold foil in a regular pattern), *harigaki* (engraving with a needle) and *tsukegaki* (raised line decoration).

The rectangular paper box with its flat lid, used for storing documents, corresponds to the *suzuribako* in its design. On the inside of the lid, an autumnal, tree-lined river landscape of towering mountains and a waterfall is accentuated by a pavilion beneath a massive cypress. The background is dominated by the snow-covered Mt. Fuji. Both two-dimensionally rendered landscapes are given atmospheric depth through finely differentiated colouring. The precise, almost empirical rendering of the landscapes blends with a traditional tiered perspective. This enchanting compositional blend is characteristic of the late Edo and Meiji periods, drawing from the Western-influenced painting trends of the late 18th and 19th centuries. This is no doubt also at play in the use of perspective – especially in the view of the palace. Conversely, the use of gold

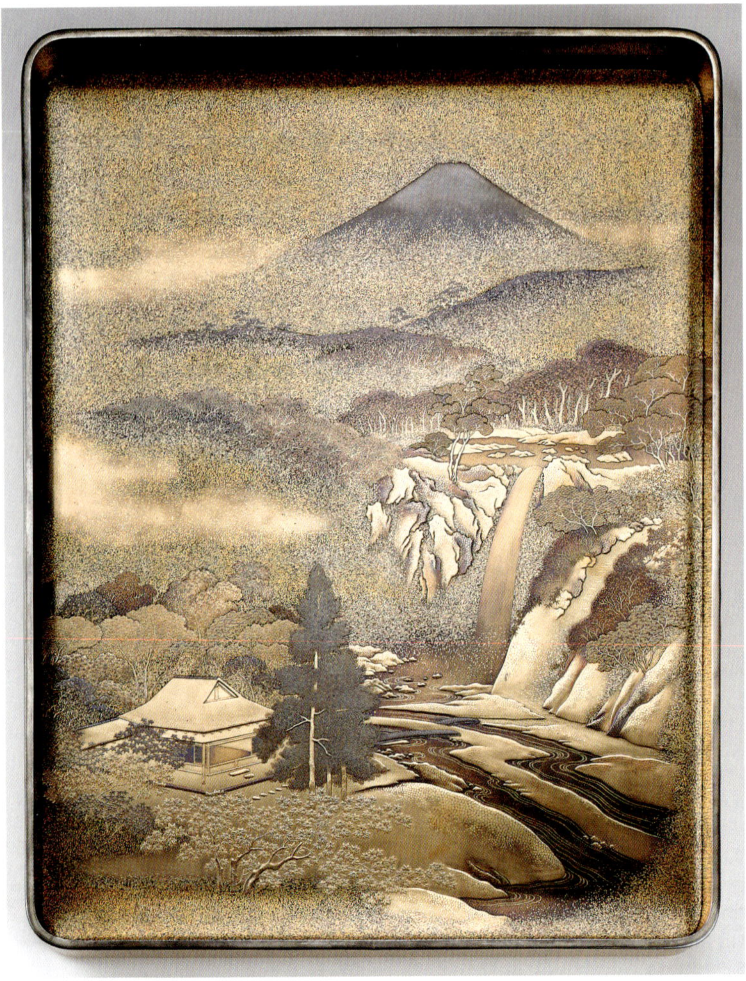

leaf to create the effect of reflected light and the modulation in the *nashiji* to create transitions are wholly traditional means of producing atmospheric density. The same is true of the random sprinkling of fine gold particles to suggest mist over mountain peaks and slopes.

Following a period of obscurity, efforts were undertaken in the Meiji period to revive the art of lacquer-work, a movement that found its greatest supporter in Emperor Meiji (r. 1868–1912). He was the most important patron of the time. Both boxes were a gift from the Emperor to Erwin von Bälz, a German physician who was professor of medicine in Tokyo (1876–1905) and was appointed personal physician to the Emperor. In form and decoration, they reflect Meiji court taste, characterized by technical perfection and the use of extremely fine gold powder.

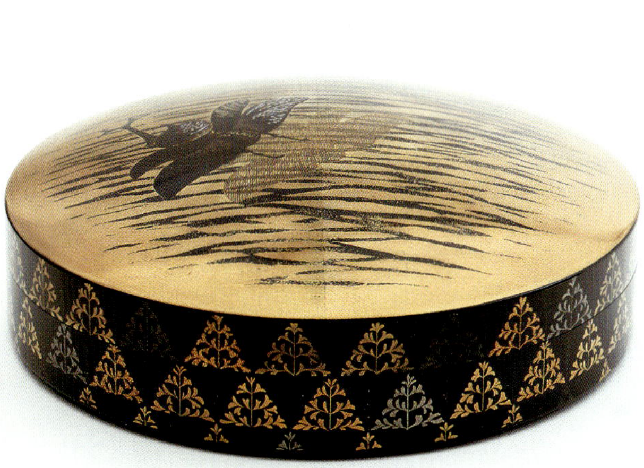

Gold lacquer box "Forest Lake"

Taguchi Yoshikuni (1923–1998)
1983
Hinoki wood, gold, silver and green lacquered *makie*, mother-of-pearl and *okibirame* on black lacquer
Height 8.8 cm, diameter 25.5 cm
Signed: Yoshikuni
Name (on storage container): *Mori no Mizuumi* ("Forest Lake")
Inv. No. 1984-7

The upright walls of the round box lid are decorated with stylized trees on a shiny black lacquered ground, sprinkled with gradations of gold and silver powder, *togidashi-makie*. The curved lid is decorated with a depiction of the gently flowing waters of a forest lake in black lacquer and silver *togidashi*. A cut-out in the shape of a flying stag beetle is set into the water surface, its dark figure of reflecting black lacquer adorned with gold foil, *okibirame*, and strips of mother-of-pearl, all strewn with the finest *makie*. The shadow of the beetle is engraved into the gold lacquer in the finest scraffito, *harigaki*. The inside of the box and lid are decorated with finely striped, gradated gold and silver *makie*. The lid was created by Taguchi Yoshikuni, commissioned by the Museum. It is brilliantly executed, both in technique and artistic style.

The combination of *makie*, engraving, and the finest mother-of-pearl inlay, as in this "Forest Lake" box, and the lyrical mood of the motif, are characteristic of Taguchi's work, which always reflects the artist's close connection to nature. Moreover, it is exemplary of the high artistic level of modern Japanese lacquerware.

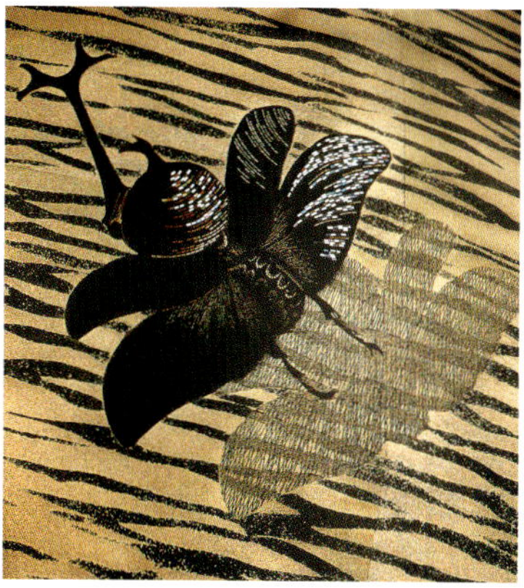

Nō mask, *ko-omote* type

Edo period, 18th century
Lacquer and colour on hinoki wood
Height 21, width 13.2 cm
Estate of Dr. Marianne Rumpf
Inv. No. 1999-24

The *ko-omote* masks (literally, "little face") embodied the ideal beauty of the Heian period and were created for graceful young women characters in *Katsura Nō*. The full, oval face tapers towards the brow and is elongated by means of the painted eyebrows positioned high on the forehead. The eyelids follow a straight line; the sight holes are oval. The nostrils are softly shaped, as is the slightly open mouth, which reveals black-tinted teeth. The lower lip is pushed forward and ends in the raised corners of the mouth, resulting in the youthful, carefree smile typical of the *ko-omote*. The cheeks are full, and the slight double chin is fashioned in a pronounced plasticity. However, the expression of lovely, internalized beauty, found in reproductions (*utsushi*) of prototypes (*honmen*) attributed to the woodcarver Tatsuemon (late 14th century), has been replaced in this mask by a coarser nuance that brings it closer to the type of mask known as *manbi* ("thousand coquetries"). This mask embodies the sensual, erotic aspects of the female characters in *Nō* theatre, developed for the first time at the beginning of the Edo period when new plays called for new types of masks.

The three fine strands of hair (*kegaki*), running parallel to the side of the head, however, are a clear indicator for the *ko-omote* mask, since they cannot be found with the *manbi* type. During the Edo period representative female masks were created for the leading female roles of the great Nō schools. For this purpose, two families, *Komparu* and *Kita*, use the *ko-omote* mask up to this day. The other schools chose *ko-omote* masks for their female supporting roles, *tsure*. This unsigned *ko-omote* is possibly a *tsure-men*.

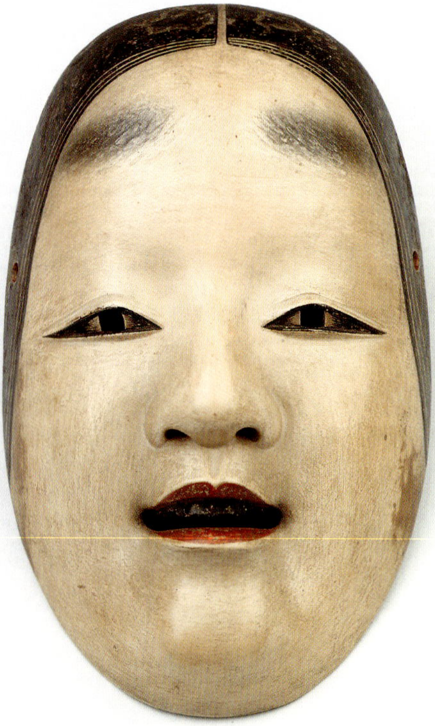

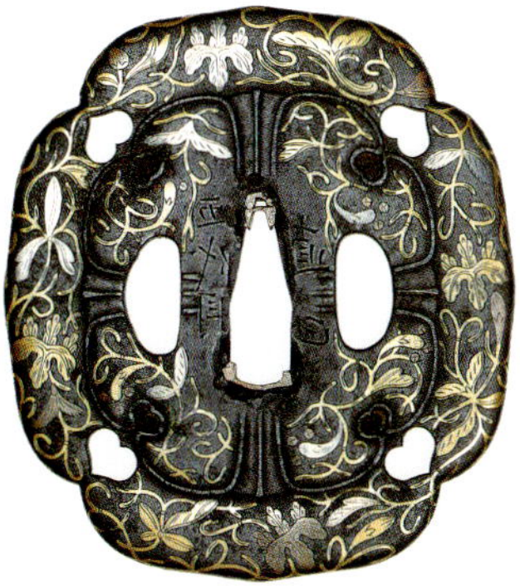

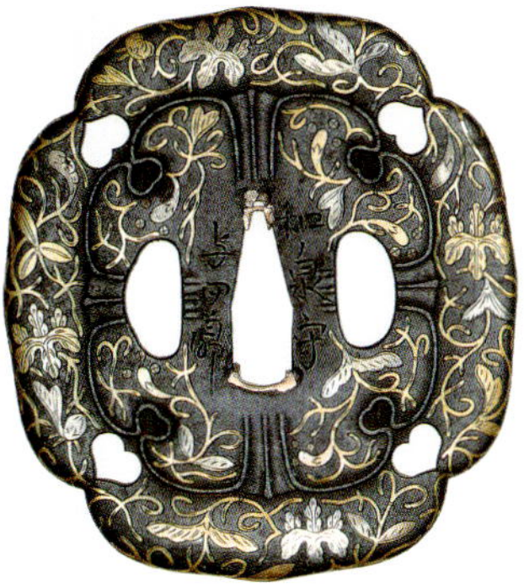

Sword guard, *tsuba*

Edo period, 18th–19th century
Iron and inlay in brass, copper, and silver
Height 8.4 cm, width 7.7 cm, depth 0.3 cm
Signature (front): *Godaime Naomasa*
(back): *Izumi no kami yoshirō*
Inv. No. 1976-22

The sword guard (*tsuba*) is usually an openwork iron or bronze disk. It shields the hand against an opponent's blow, while simultaneously balancing the sword. Over the course of the Edo period *tsuba* and other sword fittings grew increasingly decorative, at times even losing their simple functional aspect. This sword guard is made of iron forged into the shape of a mallow leaf, *aoi-kata*. The front and back are decorated with inlaid vines in brass, copper, and silver showing smaller leaf contours. Along the edge, the vines alternate with paulownia (*kiri*), also inlaid in brass, copper, and silver (*hirazōgan* technique). The scalloped corners curve in towards heart-shaped openings. To the right and left of the centre hole for the tang of the sword, there are two further openings, *hitsu*, for the *kōgai* and the *kozuka*, a small knife. The *kōgai* is a metal rod; its original function is unknown today. The *kozuka* is an approximately 12-cm knife. Partially raised metal inlay is typical of Yoshirō tsuba. The name Yoshirō is frequently found in inscriptions on the sword guards of this school, a reference, like the signature "Naomasa V" (*godaime Naomasa*), to the school's founder.

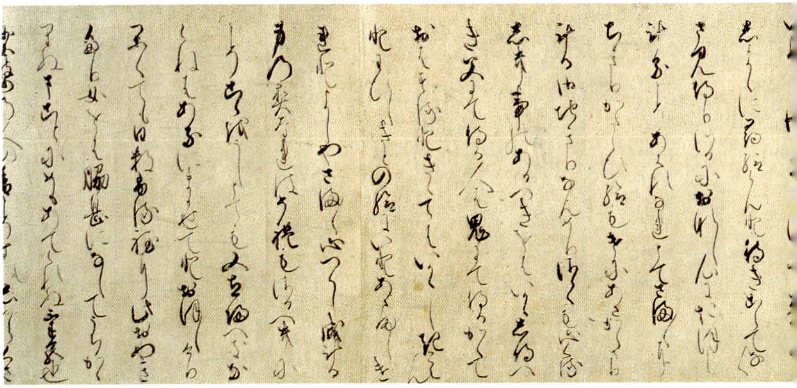

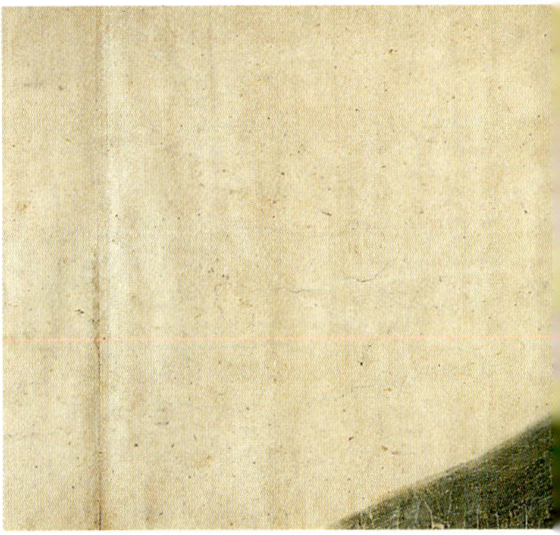

The Tale of the Young Heavenly Prince Amewakahiko

Tosa Hirochika (active ca. 1439 to 1487)
Muromachi period, 15th century
Handscroll
Ink and colour on paper
32.1 x 1046.8 cm
Inv. No. 6536

Originally composed on two handscrolls, the pictorial narrative of *Amewakahiko*, the "Young Heavenly Prince," is a combination of the fairy tale of the animal bridegroom, in truth a heavenly prince, and elements of the Chinese legend "The Cowherd and the Weaver."

The first scroll, of which only the textual parts and a 17th-century copy are extant, illustrates how the youngest daughter of a wealthy family volunteered to wed a serpent monster that was threatening her family. After the wedding, the monstrous bridegroom is revealed to be the radiant young prince Amewakahiko. But the newlyweds' happiness is short-lived, because the prince is summoned back to Heaven by his father.

The Berlin scroll, which illustrates the second part of the story, begins with the young wife's arrival in Heaven, searching for her husband. She receives help from the celestial constellations, who guide her on her way. But the couple's reunion is prevented by a demon, dispatched by the prince's father.

To remain in Heaven at her husband's side, the young woman must first perform several difficult tasks. These include guiding a herd of cattle

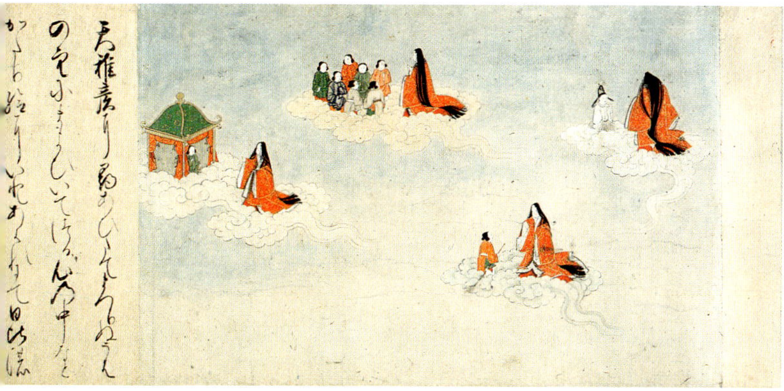

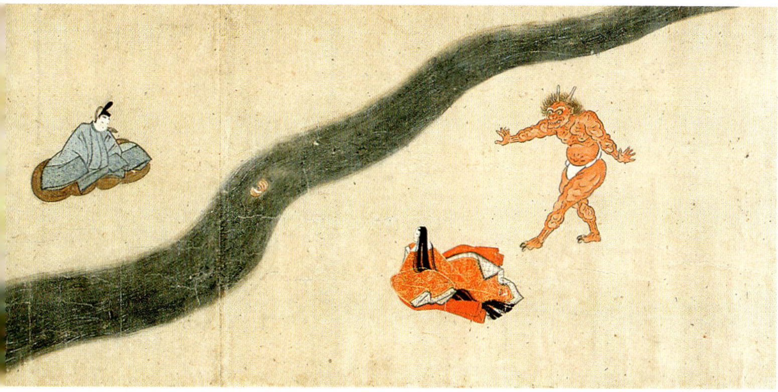

scattered across the heavens back to their stable and transferring rice from one granary to another, a kernel at a time. She is also locked in a room full of poisonous millipedes and later, a room with thousands of snakes.

But thanks to a magic garment given to her by the young prince, she bravely overcomes all obstacles. Still, the couple are unable to remain together. The demon tosses a melon between them, from the juice of which the Milky Way grows, separating the lovers from one another. Only once a year, on the seventh day of the seventh month, are they allowed to meet. This day is celebrated in Japan on July 7 with the Tanabata Festival.

The seven sections of script and image alternate and complement each other on the scroll and are of outstanding artistic quality. An inscription by Prince Sadafusa (1372–1456) at the end of the scroll identifies the painter Fujiwara Tosa Hirochika as the illustrator and Emperor Go-Hanazono (1419–1470, r. 1428–1464) as the calligrapher of the accompanying texts.

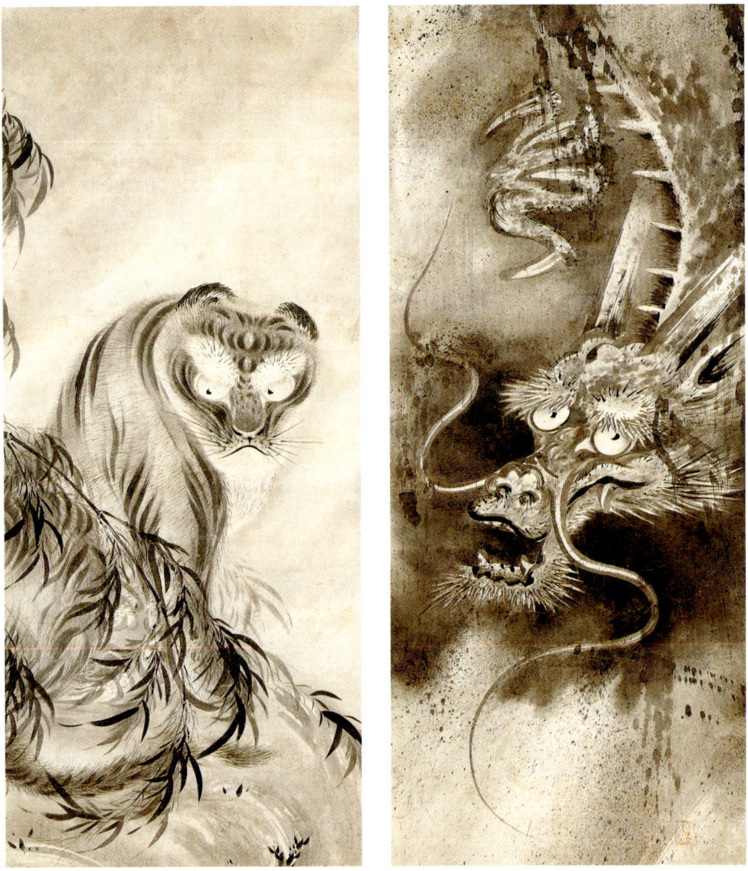

Dragon and Tiger

Oguri Sōritsu (active mid- to late 15th century)
Muromachi period, 15th century
Pair of hanging scrolls
Ink on paper, each 107.7 x 47.5 cm
Inv. No. 1980-34,35

Half hidden behind dark clouds heavy with rain, a dragon glides towards the centre of the image in a sweeping curve that follows the diagonal axis. His companion, the tiger, is rendered less dramatically, though his form is no less dynamic. Sitting on his hind legs, the tiger's supple body is turned to the right, while his gaze is directed towards the viewer with a grave and mistrustful expression.
The *Book of Changes* (C: *Yijing*), the Chinese classic, describes the dragon and the tiger as an uneven pair, symbols of the natural phenomena of rain and wind. Moreover, they embody the all-encompassing might of a ruler. Depictions of dragons and tigers were introduced to Japan during the first half of the 14th century with the arrival of Chan (J: Zen) Buddhism in Japan, where they became especially popular among Zen monks and samurai.

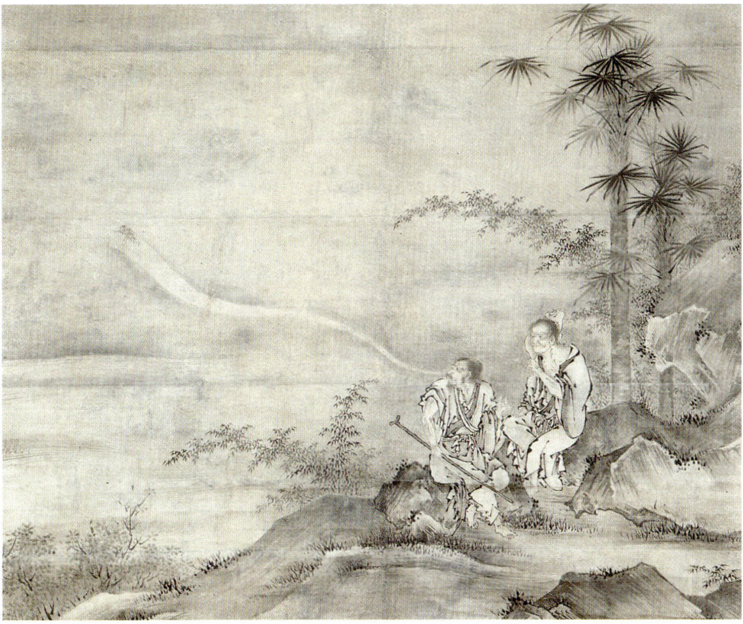

Gama Sennin and Tekkai Sennin

Kanō Motonobu's workshop
(1476–1559)
Second half of 16th century
Hanging scroll
Ink on paper, 128.7 x 157.5 cm
Inv. No. 2000-1

The immortal depicted to the right – described as Hou Xiansheng in Chinese Daoist legends – is called Gama Sennin in Japan, because he is always accompanied by a three-legged toad (J: *gama*). In addition, he is said to have had toadlike skin and a hairless face, characteristics that earned him this nickname.

The nickname Tekkai, literally "iron rod," was derived from the attribute associated with the second Daoist immortal: an iron crutch. Li Tiekuai, as Tekkai Sennin was called in Chinese, had originally been a handsome young Daoist, whose talent was so great that even Laozi (Lao Tzu) would seek his company from time to time for conversation. One day, Li Tiekuai was once again called to visit Laozi, and on this occasion he left his mortal, human body behind with a disciple who was to guard it. But the disciple was careless and misplaced Li's body, so that when he returned he had no choice but to make do with the body of an old beggar who had just died. Tekkai Sennin is always depicted as a ragged, ugly beggar with an iron crutch. His true corporeal form takes flight in the cloud of his exhaled breath.

The unusual, wide format of this scroll indicates that it was originally pasted directly on the wall in a niche and only later remounted as a hanging scroll. The severe, clean composition and the distinct brushwork point to Kanō Motonobu, the founder of the academic Kanō school. Images of the eccentric immortals Gama and Tekkai are among the most popular themes in Zen Buddhist ink painting.

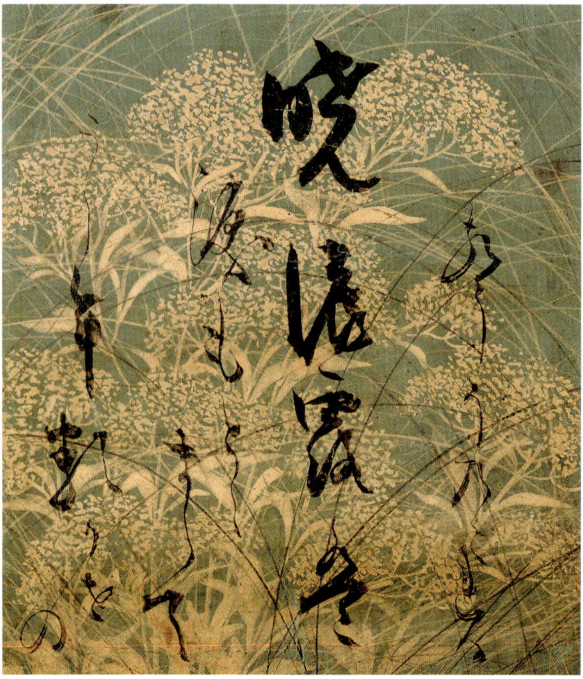

Waka Poetry and Paintings of Flowers and Grasses

Calligraphy by Hon'ami Kōetsu (1558–1637), painting in the style of Tawaraya Sōtatsu (?–1643?)
Circa 1610
Thirty-six *shikishi* album leaves
Ink, colour, gold, and silver on paper, each 18.3 x 16.2 cm
Inv. No. 243 a-b

Originally mounted on a pair of six-fold screens, the thirty-six decorated poem leaves have been remounted as album leaves. Hon'ami Kōetsu executed his selection of thirty-six waka poems taken from the *Shin-kokin wakashū* imperial anthology in a lively cursive script, scattered over painting in the style of Tawaraya Sōtatsu. Flower, grass, and landscape motifs reflect the four seasons. They are painted in gold and silver in the so-called "boneless" technique. The creator of this type of underpainting is generally thought to be Tawaraya Sōtatsu, the founder of the Japanese decorative painting tradition known as *Rinpa*, in collaboration with the artists in his studio. Kōetsu's exquisite calligraphy and Sōtatsu's genius in pictorial design combine to create an exquisitely harmonious work of art.

The illustration shows *ominaeshi* blossoms and autumn grasses. The poem was written by the court lady Sagamì, Oto Jijū, in the 11th century:

At dawn when we must part,
Dew and my tears,
Fall ceaselessly.
Thundering in the distance,
The nocturnal wind is left behind,
alone.

The Tale of the Heike

Unknown master of the Tosa school
Edo period, 17th century
Fan-shaped album leaf
Ink and colour on paper with gold ground, 59 illustrations and 60 texts, each 11.3 x 24.8 cm
Inv. No. 1969-10

The literary source for these illustrations is Japan's most famous heroic epic, *Heike monogatari*, which describes the battles between the rival Taira and Minamoto clans fighting for political supremacy in 12th-century Japan.

With the utmost delicate brushwork and the highest degree of care in rendering details such as fabric patterns, features, and gestures, and by using precious pigments and gold paint, the unknown artist has brought the individual episodes to life. In so doing, he expertly adapted his compositions to the shape of the fan. Decorative bands of clouds in opaque gold provide the spatial frame for each scene.

The image reproduced on this page illustrates Chapter 11 of Book 3, "Debate about the Doctor's Visit." The painter employed a manner of composition common to the Japanese painting style known as *yamato-e*, in which roofs, or ceilings, were "blown away" (*fukinuki yatai*) to reveal the activities in an interior.

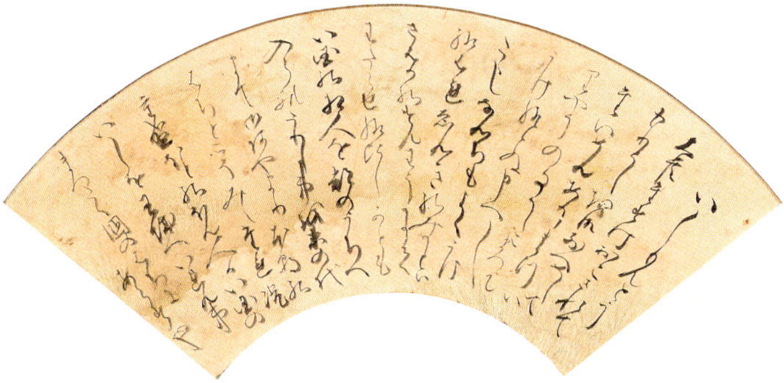

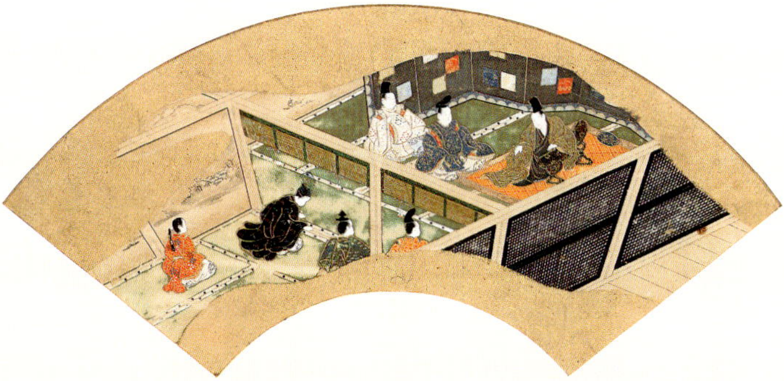

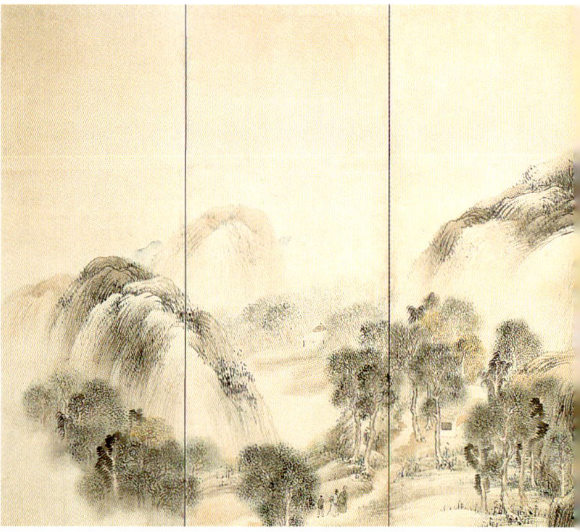

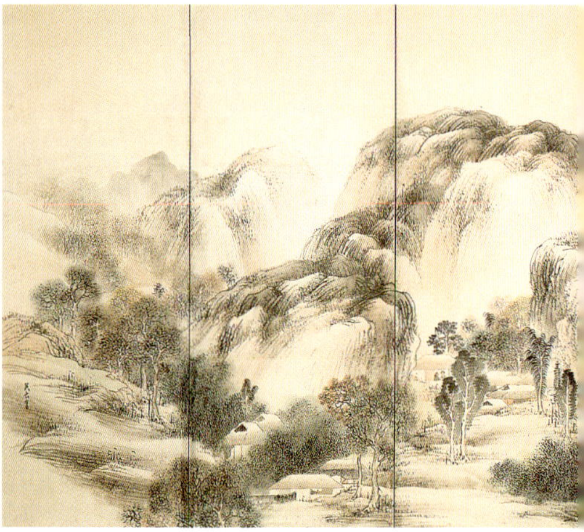

Landscape

Matsumura Goshun (1752–1811)
Circa 1781–1789
Pair of six-fold screens
Ink and light colour on paper, each 153.2 x 357.6 cm
Inv. No. 1972-7a/b

Small settlements are nestled between the tall mountain range in the background and the gently rolling hills and clusters of trees in the foreground. Isolated figures engaged in everyday activities animate the idyllic, rural scene. With the structuring "hemp-fiber" brushstrokes and rhythmically placed "moss dots," characteristic of the Literati style of painting, the artist has invested the solid masses of earth with plasticity and volume. Subtle ochre-brown and light-green washes suggest early spring, giving the image an alluring freshness; the delicate colouring creates a lyrical atmosphere.

Matsumura Gekkei studied painting and *haikai* poetry from 1781 onwards with the famous Literati painter Yosa Buson (1716–1783). In 1781 Gekkei moved from Kyoto to Ikeda, a small town near Osaka, where he remained until 1789. It was during this period that he took the pseudonym Goshun, derived from the ancient name for Ikeda.

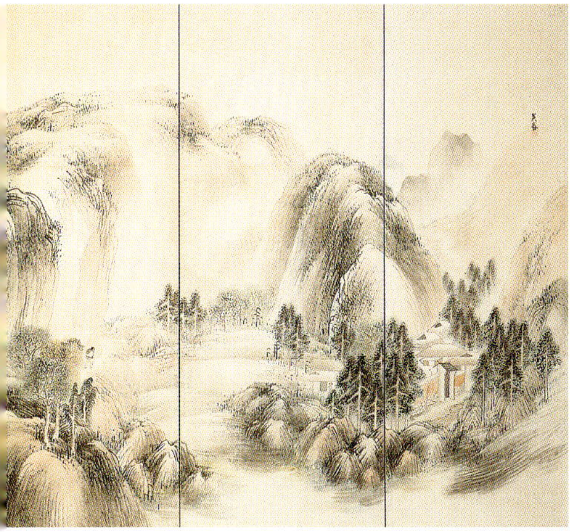

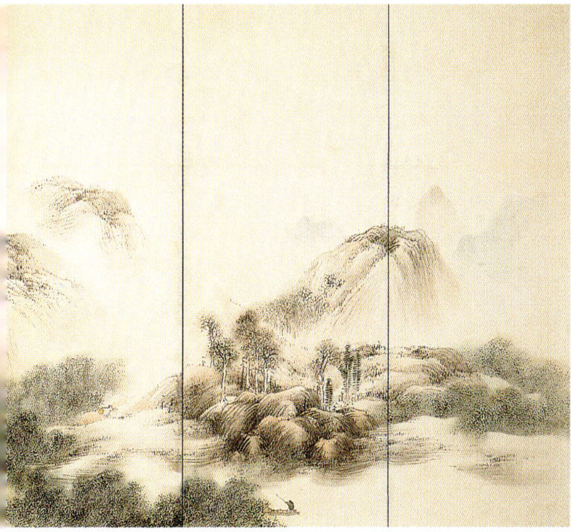

The pair of screens presented here are among the most representative of this early period, in which Buson's influence was most evident. The treatment of rocks and the characterization of figures are especially reminiscent of the master's style. Goshun's tendency towards lyricism, which marks his work, is already developed in this early piece.

Following his return to Kyoto from Ikeda in 1788–1789, Goshun joined the studio of the tremendously popular painter Maruyama Ōkyo (1733 to 1795). From Ōkyo, Goshun adopted a naturalistic, decorative style and successfully combined it with the elements of Literati painting he had studied under Buson. After Ōkyo's death in 1795, Goshun opened his own studio on Shijō street in Kyoto; his school was thus known as the Shijō school.

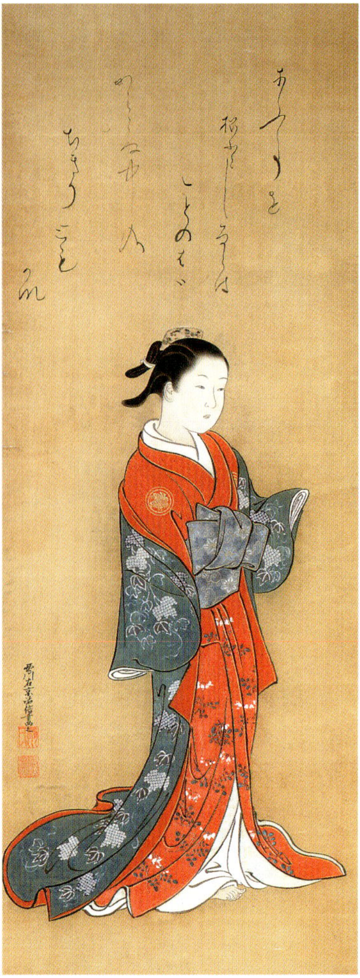

Waiting Beauty

Nishikawa Sukenobu (1671–1750)
Circa 1736–1747
Hanging scroll
Colour and gold on silk
158.2 x 41.1 cm
Klaus F. Naumann Collection

Nishikawa Sukenobu was considered the most accomplished and influential painter of the "floating world" in Kyoto during the first half of the 18th century. His staggering productivity as a book illustrator carried his fame all the way to Edo. Sukenobu's style is marked by the restrained elegance of his figures, which are rather delicate with gentle, sweet features.

The beauty portrayed on this scroll is dressed in a blue overgarment, *uchikake*, with an ivy pattern partially rendered in the *shibori* (tie-dye) technique over a red kimono decorated with bush clover. The overgarment reveals the house crest of the courtesan: a swallowtail set in a double circle. The sash, which matches the overgarment in colour, is artfully tied at the front and decorated with the flowers and leaves of a clematis.

The accompanying poem, written in a fluid style with a fine brush, was most likely composed by the courtesan herself. It reads:

I know
To meet him
Means to wait.
Yet his words are a
Promise of eternal love!

Beauties in the Capital in Summer and Winter

Utagawa Toyohiro (1773–1828)
Circa 1789–1801
Pair of hanging scrolls
Colour on silk, each 100 x 39.4 cm
Inv. No. 2636 a/b

The hanging scroll on the right depicts a courtesan and her maid in animated conversation as they stroll along the Sumida River. Dressed in breezy, light summer kimono, they act as repoussoir to the water surface that reaches into the depth of the image and is ruffled by a slight breeze. The scene on the left hanging

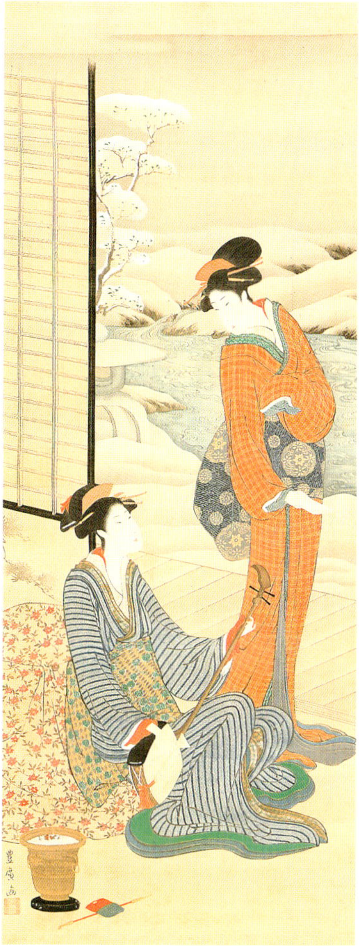 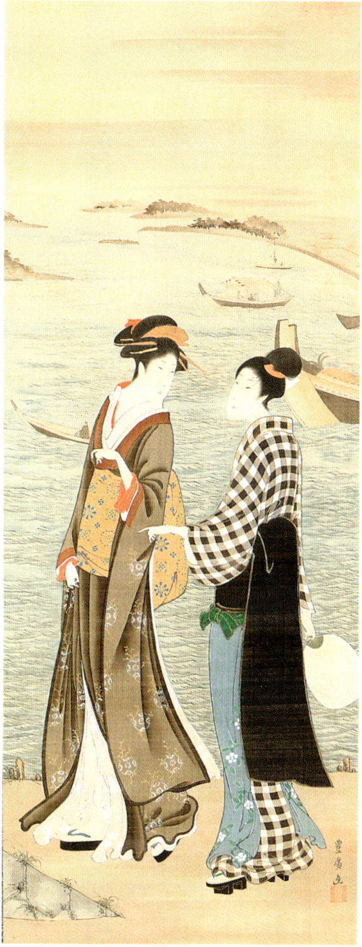

scroll shows an interior. A courtesan is seated on the floor, her back resting against a *kotatsu* table as she plays a *shamisen*. In the foreground, we see a *hibachi* filled with coals, her smoking utensils on the floor nearby. A second courtesan seems to pause on her way past. She turns around slightly, gazing down at her colleague, perhaps to comment on her playing. An open sliding door reveals a garden with an artificial watercourse. The stone lantern, the trees, and the ground are covered in a thick blanket of snow.

Next to Utagawa Toyokuni I (1769–1825), Toyohiro was one of the most eminent students of the innovative woodblock print master Utagawa Toyoharu (1735–1814). In contrast to the extroverted Toyokuni, Toyohiro was regarded as an introverted, morose individual. This character trait is evident in the melancholy, lyrical mood of his work.

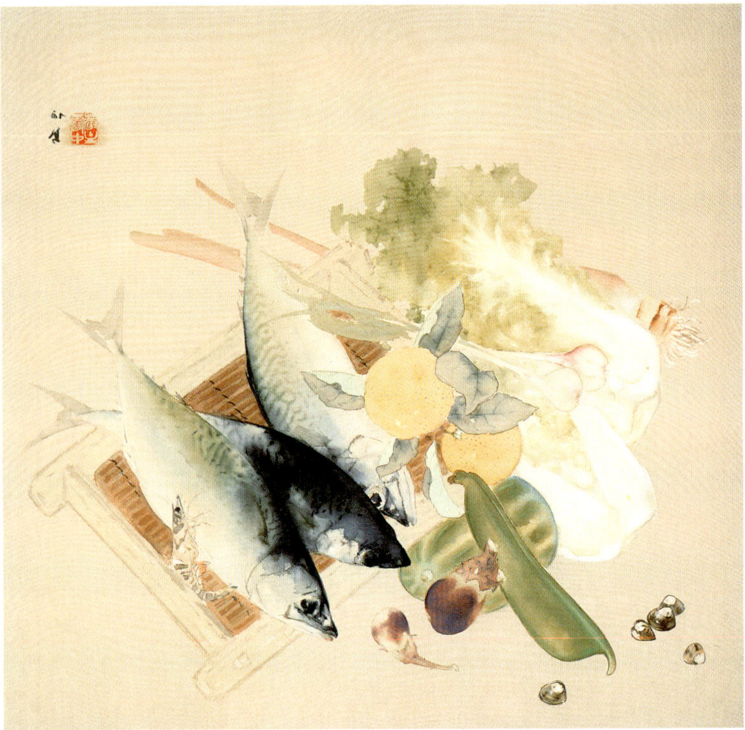

Still Life with Fish and Vegetables

Takeuchi Seihō (1864–1942)
1930
Framed *Nihonga* painting
Colour on silk, 68 x 73 cm
Inv. No. 5839

Takeuchi Seihō, a major figure in the *nihonga* painting tradition in Kyoto at the beginning of the 20th century, studied at first under Kono Bairei (1844–1895), the last prominent representative of the Maruyama-Shijō school.

During a trip to Europe at the end of the 19th century, Seihō saw the works of Corot and Turner and was profoundly impressed by them. Upon his return to Japan in 1900, Seihō developed with varying degrees of success a technique of colour washes, which came very close to European watercolour painting. It was at this time that he replaced the first character of his name, *sei*, with a homonym meaning "west" or "the West."

From 1925 onwards, Takeuchi Seihō travelled frequently to Numazu, a seaside resort on the Izu peninsula, where he visited a friend. The local culinary specialities inspired many of his compositions. Since his family also ran a fish restaurant in Kyoto, Seihō was always interested in depicting the fresh ingredients of a gourmet kitchen.

This still life is a harmonious synthesis of the Japanese Maruyama-Shijō school, with its emphasis on sketching from nature and gently lyrical atmosphere, and the Western technique of watercolour painting.

Valley in Mist

Higashiyama Kaii (1908–1999)
1989
Framed *Nihonga* painting
Colour on paper, 92 x 65 cm
Inv. No. 1989-14

Mountain landscapes veiled in mist are a recurring theme in the work of Higashiyama Kaii, considered one of the foremost artists of 20th-century Japan. The strong linear clarity of the composition is characteristic of his landscapes. In this image, rows of trees cross the image on a diagonal, the parallel arrangement leading the eye deep into the narrow valley. The meditative, somewhat melancholic atmosphere is also typical of Higashiyama's oeuvre.

The first impression of a spare monochromatic image on closer examination yields to recognition of Higashiyama Kaii's masterful gradation of tonalities, bringing the blue-grey pigments alive in an intense luminosity.

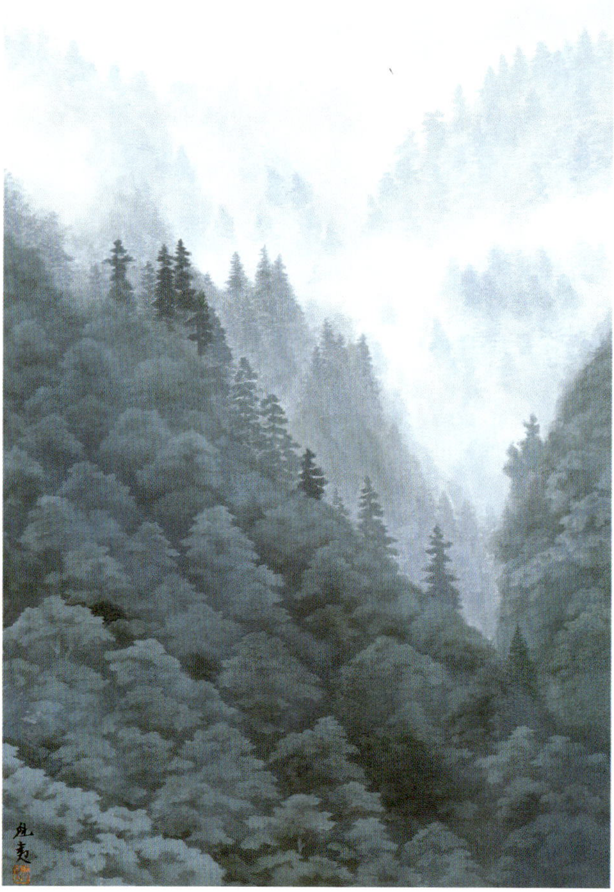

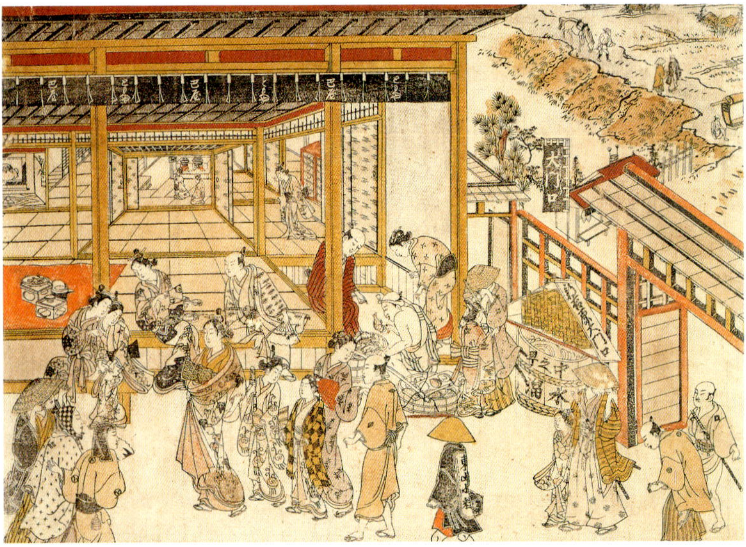

Main Entrance to the Shin-Yoshiwara Pleasure Quarters

Ōkumura Masanobu
(ca. 1686–1764)
Late 1740s
Hand-coloured print (*beni-e*)
Ōban format 30.3 x 42.5 cm
(trimmed)
Collector's seal on back: *Strauß-Negbaur*
Inv. No. 6002-28.51

The animated square in front of the main gate to Shin-Yoshiwara spreads before the viewer's eyes like a stage, with the teahouse Tomoeya in the background. Life in the pleasure quarters is illustrated with a sure hand for humor and detail: while guests are being greeted in the foreground at the gate, a courtesan strolls by flanked by her servants. Some samurai, intent on preserving their anonymity, have pulled traveller's straw hats over their faces. In the background, merchants offer their goods for sale. The sliding walls of the teahouse have been removed to provide a view into the interior, where a courtesan and her guest have settled in the middle room. The kitchen is visible in the rear wing. In a side room a girl dressed in a *furisode* kimono awaits a visitor. Outside the gate, a banner proclaims "Main Entrance to the New Yoshiwara."

Okumura Masanobu was both a woodblock artist and a publisher. He was active at a time of innovation in woodblock printing, culminating in the elaborate and expensive multi-coloured prints of Harunobu in 1765. Masanobu was the first artist to create so-called *uki-e* (perspective images) in the 1740s. These works clearly betray his study of perspective drawing in the European manner, a style that appeared odd to the Japanese eye at first. Masanobu produced many of his perspective images as *beni-e*. In addition to *beni* (a deep pink colour obtained from saffron, fading to pink), they were often hand-coloured with other natural dyes.

"Wild Geese Alighting on a Koto"

Suzuki Harunobu (1724–1770)
1765–66
From the series "Eight Views of Interiors"
Colour print
28.4 x 20.9 cm
Inv. No. 6010-04.355

This series of eight images is an ironic variation on the classic Chinese landscape painting theme "The Eight Views of Xiao and Xiang." Since the Muromachi period, this theme was also included in the repertory of Japanese artists. Around 1500 it even became fully Japanese: in reference to the Chinese model, eight picturesque scenes from villages around Lake Biwa in Omi province were chosen. In the woodblock art of the Edo period, whose subjects were often drawn from the pleasure quarters, woodcarving masters once again returned to this classic motif, albeit in an ironic manner. Instead of landscapes, life in the Yoshiwara teahouses now provided the setting.

In this print, the courtesan dressed in an elaborate kimono is getting ready to play the koto, a Japanese zither. A servant, seated diagonally across from her, is selecting an appropriate piece of music from a stack of notebooks. The black, V-shaped frets of the koto are no doubt intended as an allusion to wild geese alighting. This corresponds to the first scene in the classic version: "Wild Geese Alighting on Sandbanks."

Although Harunobu is not named in the composition, his style is evident in the spare elegance of the image. Harunobu's subtle lines and colouring, as well as the androgynous figures, had a lasting influence on the early masters of woodcarving. In addition, his greatest artistic contribution was the invention of the registered printing block, which made multicoloured woodblock printing possible.

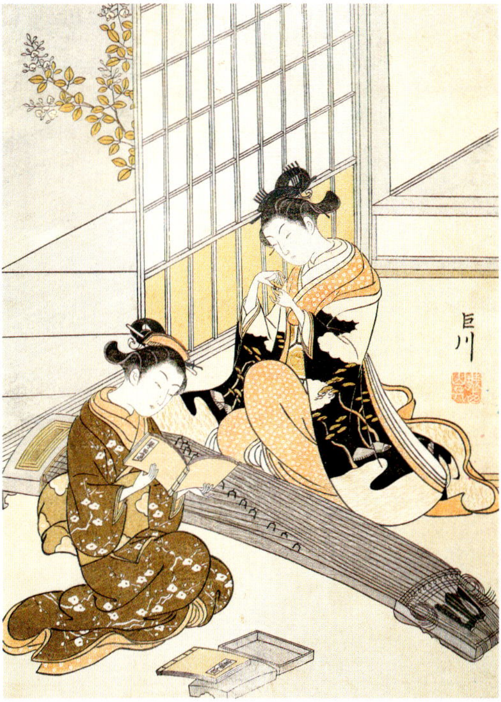

Girl with Cat

Isoda Koryūsai
(active ca. 1764–1788)
1870s
Colour (*nishiki-e*) pillar print (*hashira-e*), 72.4 x 12.3 cm
Signed: *Koryūsai ga*
Inv. No. 60025-04.415

Startled, a girl looks at a cat clawing at her white-patterned ochre *furisode* kimono with a pale yellow undergarment. As if suppressing a scream, she lifts her right hand to her mouth. Behind the girl is a pillar. From the ceiling, a vase with a flower arrangement is visible. The motif of the girl with a playful cat is a reference to Chapter 34 of *The Tale of Genji*. The chapter contains a scene in which Princess Nyosan, the wife of Prince Genji, hides behind a curtain and secretly watches the courtiers playing a game of soccer. When a cat pulls down the curtain, one of the courtiers, Kashiwagi, catches a glimpse of the princess. Thus begins a love story with an unhappy ending. In this image, the princess is transformed into a girl in contemporary costume.

Koryūsai was a leading artist of the *ukiyo-e* style. His biographical data are not known. One of his signatures contains the description *bukō* (samurai) with which he emphasized his illustious background, even though he had been dismissed from service by his feudal lord Tsuchiya and had moved to Edo as a *rōnin* (masterless samurai). Isoda Koryūsai was a friend of Suzuki Harunobu (ca. 1724 to 1770), the leading master of woodblock prints of his day, and was strongly influenced by his friend's style. Harunobu's childlike and graceful female figures recur in Koryūsai's rendering of female figures in his early paintings and woodblock prints. During this period, the artist signed his work Koryūsai Haruhiro. By the mid-1870s he had developed his own style. His figures are more solid and realistic, as is the palette in which olive green and *tan* orange set the accents. Koryūsai's female figures with their *tōrōbin* ("lantern hairstyle") set the fashion in the pleasure quarters of Edo. He is famous for his series of more than a hundred sheets entitled "New Models, Fresh as Young Leaves," which date to the end of the 1870s. Isoda Koryūsai created masterful compositions in the narrow, vertical format of the pillar prints (*hashira-e*). In the example shown here he achieves a spatial rendition of foreground and background, of width and depth, by cutting the figure off at the margin, by the diagonal direction of the ceiling beams and the veranda planks, all despite the limiting format of the print. Koryūsai's images are reminiscent of the Kano style. After 1781 he focused exclusively on *ukiyo-e* paintings and gave up woodblock printing.

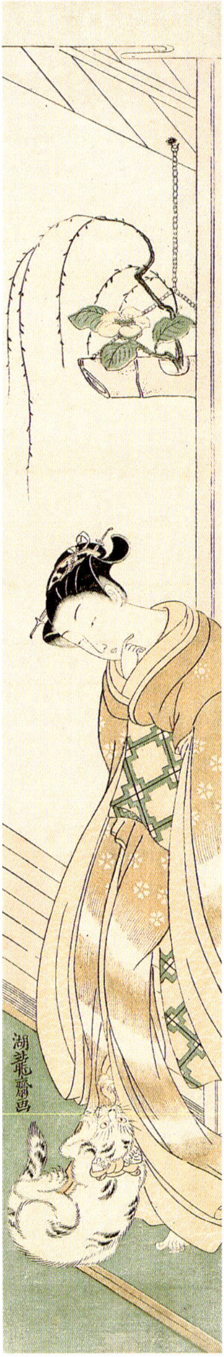

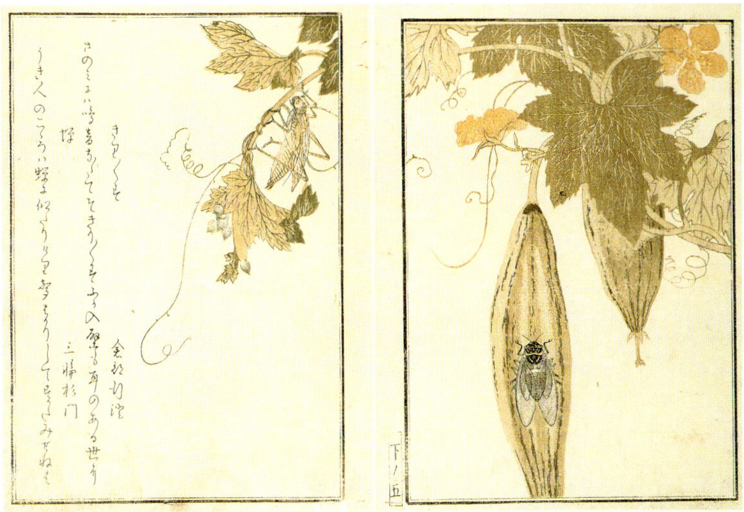

"Picture Book of Selected Insects"

Kitagawa Utamaro (1753–1806)
Colour print (*nishiki-e*)
1787
27.3 x 33.4 cm
Inv. No. 6120-04.626

In 1787, the two-volume woodblock book *Ehon Mushi Erabi* was published with fifteen double-page illustrations by Utamaro of insects and plants accompanied by humorous poems (*kyōka*) by well-known poets. In the foreword, the poet Yadoya no Meshimori (1753–1830) mentions an illustrated volume of poetry on insects compiled by Kinoshita Chōshōshi (1569–1649) in the 17th century. Utamaro was probably inspired by this earlier volume. Page 13 features a drawing of a grasshopper (*kirigirisu*) and a cicada (*semi*) on a black-spotted cucumber gourd (*hechima*). The following poems are set as commentary on the insects:

Sanomi niwa
Nakine na tatezo
Kirigirisu
Fukairu kabe mo
Mimi no aru yo ni
— Kurabe no Yukisumi

Grasshopper,
Don't chirp so loudly
For all your secrets may be heard!
If you are making love,
Be wary, for even the walls
have ears

Uki hito no
Kokoro wa semi ni
Nitari keri
Koe bakari shite
Sugata misenaba
— Miwa no Sugikado

Oh! A cold-hearted person
If like a cicada,
Which can be heard
But
Is nowhere to be seen.

The high quality of the print is proof of the esteem Utamaro's publisher Tsutaya Jūsaborō (1748–1997) had for the artist's work. In the afterword, Toriyama Sekien (1712–1788), Utamaro's teacher, draws the reader's attention to the skill of the woodcarver Tōissō. He goes on to mention how Utamaro noticed and observed details even as a child and draws a complimentary comparison in reference to the theme of the volume between Utamaro's artistic style and the behaviour of insects.

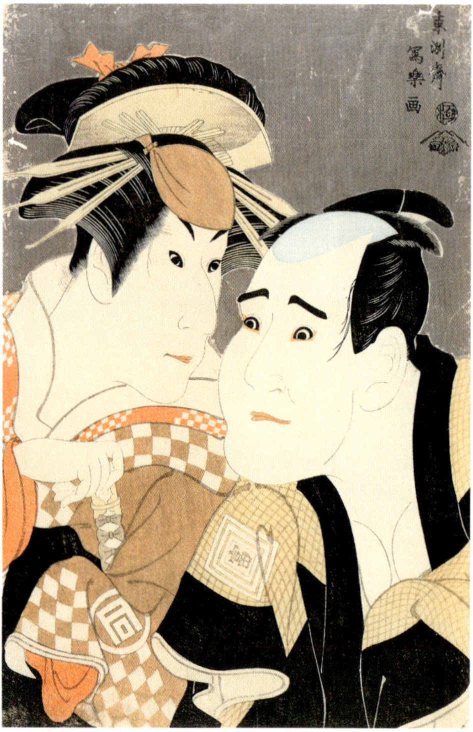

The Actors Sanokawa Ichimatsu III and Ichikawa Tomiemon

Tōshūsai Sharaku (active 1794–1795)
Portraits (*okubi-e*)
Colour print (*nishiki-e*) on
mica ground, 1794
Ōban format 37.7 x 25.4 cm
Signed: *Tōshōsai Sharaku ga*; Publisher: Tsuta-ya Jūsaburō (colophon)
Censor seal: *kiwame*
Inv. No. 6155-04.428

During the ten months of his recorded activity, Tōshūsai Sharaku created some 150 prints of actors and wrestlers, of which 144 have been traced. Little is known of the artist's life. He is said to have been a *Nō* actor called Saitō Jūrobei. According to a contemporary publication, the *Ukiyo-e Ruikō*, Sharaku was severely criticized. One reason was the expressive, psychological realism with which he revealed the character of those he depicted. It is precisely for this trait that Sharaku is highly appreciated today. His "close-up portraits," *okubi-e*, are regarded as a high point in woodblock printing. Dark mica-dust ground, as in the background of this print, was employed for the first time by Sharaku. Among the few double portraits by Sharaku, this is the only to show a man and a woman (though both are in fact male actors). The narrow, determined face of Ichimatsu in the role of the Gion courtesan Onayo Hakujin stands in strong contrast to the timid, plump face of Tomiemon as the scoundrel Kanisaka Tōma in the play *Hana-ayame Bunroku Soga*, performed in Edo from May 1794 onwards. Strong lines portray not only the character of each role, but also the individuality of the actors. The role of Onayo was defined by Sanokawa Ichimatsu I and ever since, it has been performed in a kimono with a checkered border, as shown here. Sharaku also created a single portrait of Sanokawa Ichimatsu III (1759 to 1813) in this role. Only four examples of this print are thought to have survived, one of which is housed in the National Museum in Tokyo.

Amida Falls in the Mountains of Kiso

Katsushika Hokusai (1760–1849)
Title of series: "The Waterfalls of Various Provinces"
Circa 1833
Colour print (*nishiki-e*)
Ōban format 36.9 x 25.5 cm
Signed: *Zen Hokusai Iitsu hitsu*
Publisher: Eijudō (Nishimura-ya Yohachi)
Inv. No. 6205-E1037

In clear, glowing colours this portrait-format print shows Amida Falls, which owes its name to an opening in the rock through which a mountain lake plunges into the depths. The nearly circular shape of the opening is reminiscent of the head of Amida Buddha. Steep cliffs with dense growth frame the spectacular panorama. Two travellers have settled down for a picnic on a rocky overlook; their servant is engaged in preparing tea. The title in the left cartouche reads "Amida Falls at the Kiso Highway Mountain Pass." The print is one of a series of eight which Hokusai created even as he was still occupied with drawing the famous series "Thirty-six Views of Mt. Fuji." Hokusai was one of the most versatile artists in Japan's history.

The painter and graphic artist left more than 30,000 drawings and woodcuts. He was remarkable for his extraordinary talent in draughtsmanship and his independent approach to depicting landscapes. His "Sketches" (*manga*), which he published from 1819 onwards, are famous. Throughout his life he worked with a great variety of stylistic traditions and technical challenges. The sure-handed treatment of these challenges led the "Mad-About-Painting Old Man," as he signed himself in his woodcuts after 1833, to develop a unique, memorable style which always captured the essential aspect of a shape, an expression, or a mood.

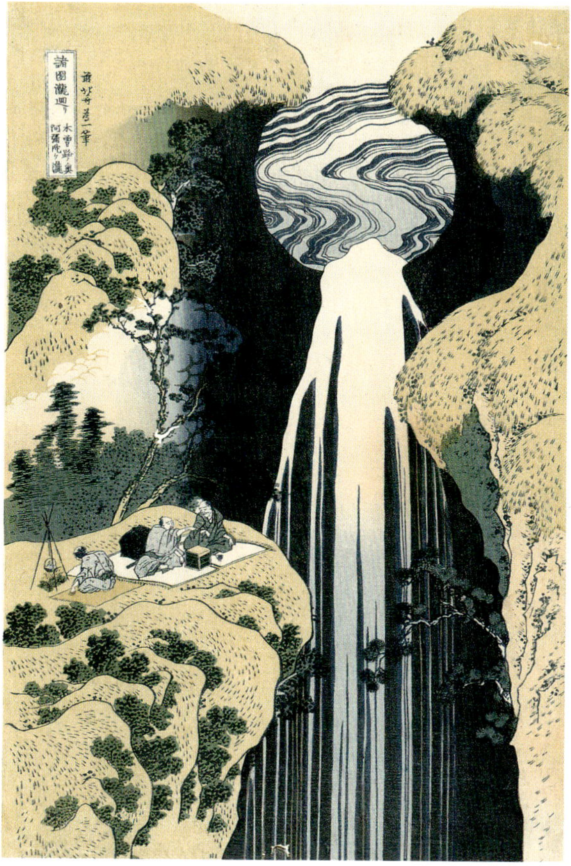

White Rooster on Drum

Totoya Hokkei (1780–1850)
1825 (later print)
Surimono with gold and silver onlays (*kinginzuri*) and blind printing (*karazuri*)
Signed: *Aoigaoka Hokkei*
21.1 x 18.2 cm
Meyer-Große Bequest, 1919
Inv. No. 6265-19.233

Surimono ("printed matter") were published from the mid-19th century onwards in small editions as luxurious woodblock prints used for gifts. A pictorial calendar, *egoyomi*, in this privately printed *surimono* indicates the year 1825 in the form of a rooster as the zodiac sign, with the months being indicated on the drum. In addition, the rooster on the ivy-covered drum is a symbol of peace, an allusion to a Chinese legend according to which the war drum slipped into obscurity during the peaceful reign of the mythical Emperor Yao (3rd millennium BC). The drum was overgrown by plants and chickens came to roost on it. The poem by Suidō Gyōkei claims that the cry of roosters competing with one another can be heard from a thousand villages. Totoya Hokkei, originally a fish merchant, studied under the Kano painter Yōsen'in (1753–1808) and later with Katsushika Hokusai (1760–1849). He is considered one of the most accomplished *surimono* masters of the early 19th century. In addition to private commissions for prints, he also illustrated anthologies of humorous poems, *kyōka*, and created commercial woodblock prints. A second print in the Folk Art Museum in Leiden shows different contours in the plumage of the rooster. Since that print is a first edition, the Berlin print may be from a later edition.

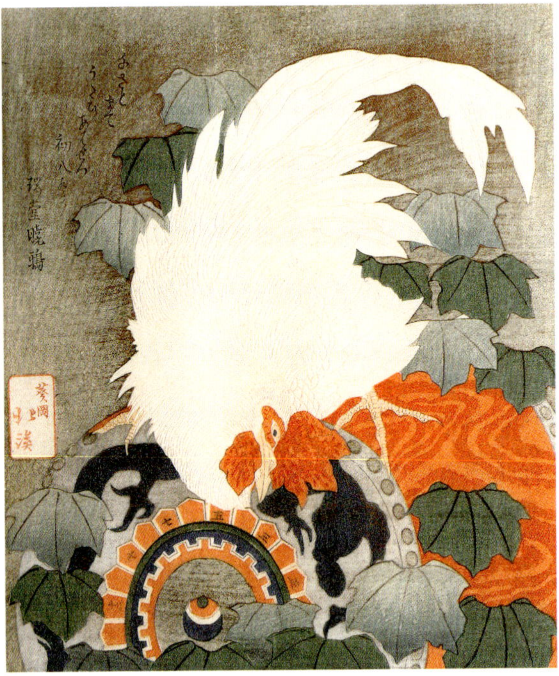

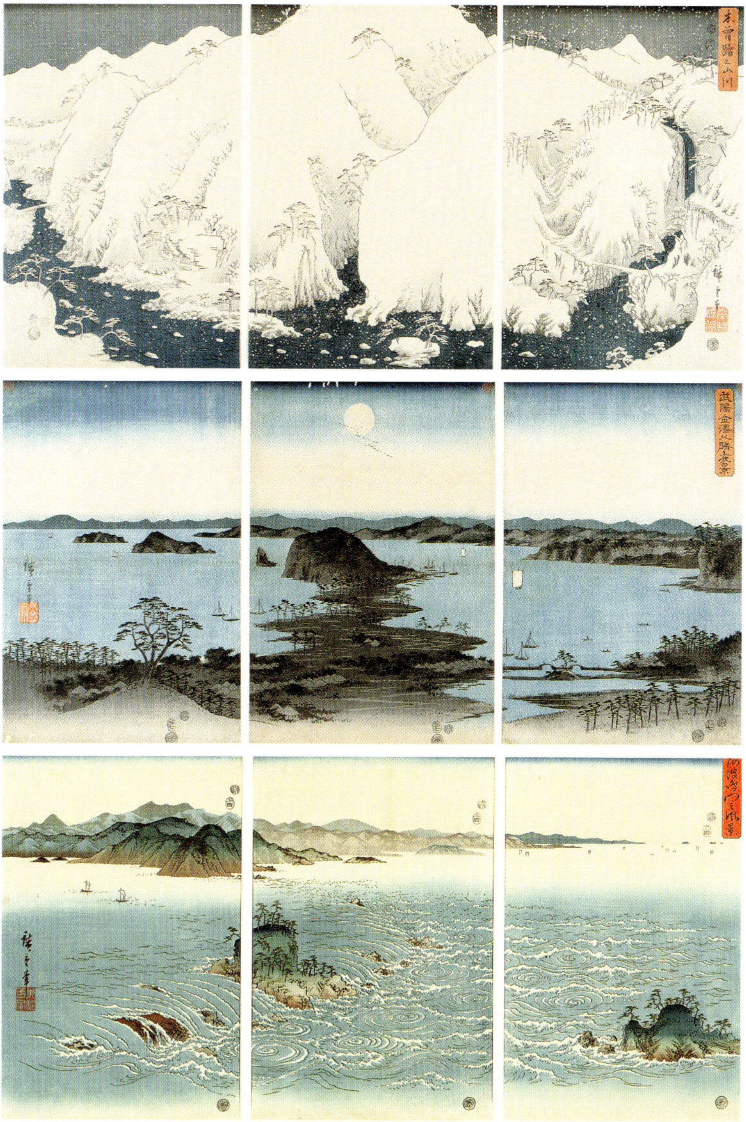

Mountains and Rivers on the Kiso Road
Evening View of Eight Famous Sites at Kanazawa
Landscape with the Whirlpools at Awa

Andō Hiroshige (1797–1858)
Colour prints

Three triptychs of Ōban format:
36-36.1 x 24.5-24.9 cm,
35.8-36 x 24.6- 24.8 cm and
36-36,2 x 24,4-24,8 cm
Signed: *Hiroshige hitsu*
Seal: *Bokurin Shōsha* (?) and *Ichiyrūsai*
Publisher: Tsutaya; censor seal (on each sheet): *aratame*

Date seal (on each sheet): sign of the snake, fourth month (1857)
Inv. No. 60080-31.35/60080-30.23/60080-04.449

At the height of his late oeuvre, Hiroshige created a series of three monumental landscape panoramas, designed as triptychs. "Snow, Moon, Cherry Blossoms" (*setsugekka*) is a traditional theme in Chinese art, an allusion to a line in a poem by the Tang period Chinese poet Bo Juyi (772–846): "In snow, moon, and cherry blossoms, I think of you." While the foam-covered eddies in the ocean narrows can be interpreted as a metaphor for the froth of cherry blossoms in spring in the triptych of the whirlpool at Naruto, Hiroshige employed realistic renditions of snow-blanketed and moonlit landscapes in the other two triptychs. The mountains peaks along the upper Kiso River rise powerfully into the sky and push far into the foreground. Spatial depth is provided by a small piece of the horizon and the river at the foot of the mountains. The impenetrable winter landscape seems untouched; only a few bridges, paths, and snow-covered houses suggest that this is an important mountain pass on the road between Edo and Kyoto. Hiroshige has organized the mountain panorama in a fairly traditional manner in terms of composition and drawing. The snow-covered pines in the foreground seem remote; only where canyons and valleys are shown do freely rendered details provide some relief from the expanse of white mountain slopes. The narrow mountain paths that meander past majestic rock cliffs direct the eye of the viewer into the distance. In the evening view of Kanazawa, Andō Hiroshige picks up on another traditional theme, the "Eight Views." Chinese in origin as well, the "Eight Views of Xiao and Xiang," *shōshō hakkei*, was incorporated into Japanese art beginning in the Muromachi period. In 1677, the "Eight Famous Sites at Kanazawa" in Musashi province were compiled for the first time. In contrast to the Kiso triptych, the evening view of Kanazawa can be grasped in one viewing. It is evident that Hiroshige was familiar with Western perspective. The evening shoreline opens onto a broad horizon in the distance. Pines line the shore and a wide spit of land occupies the middle image. There, a massive boulder juts out of the sea and guides the eye to the islands behind and on to the gentle contour of a mountain chain that stretches across the entire horizon. A few masterfully placed counter-directional elements maintain the tension in the horizontal plane. The vertical movement of the spit of land extending into the sea is accentuated by the clear light of the full moon, while a flock of birds flying in zigzag formation leads the eye to the diagonal coastline on the right margin. Hiroshige's unique style is evident even in earlier landscape series, such as "Eight Views of Ōmi," which he created soon after his successful series "Fifty-three Stations of the Tōkaidō Road" in 1833. His delicate colouring, fluid shading, *fukibokashi*, and manner of depicting fields without contour result in landscapes with a strong, painterly character. In these "true landscapes" based on nature and the changing moods of daytime and season, Hiroshige distances himself from the spectacular, dramatic landscape designs of the other leading woodcut artist of the 19th century, Katsushika Hokusai (1760–1849). The *setsugekka* motif has been visited by many woodcut artists, such as Okumura Masanobu circa 1720, and its popularity in Japanese art endured well into the late 19th century.

Portrait of Munakata Shikō

Sekino Jun'ichirō (1914–1988)
Colour print, 69/118, 1 969
77 x 63.2 cm
Mirror image: 66.4 x 53.1 cm
Red seal to the right: *Jun*
Inscription, bottom right:
Jun
Watermark: *Jun Sekino*
Inv. No. 1971-34

Sekino Jun'ichirō – like the woodcut master Munakata Shikō in this portrait – is one of the best-known *sōsaku-hanga* ("creative print") artists, who found their artistic medium in the woodcut at the beginning of the 20th century, independent of commercial requirements set by publishers. Although many artists in the Creative Print Association were trained in Western painting styles, the more familiar genre of the woodcut offered them the means to translate their artistic intent in an authentic manner.

This portrait of Munakata Shikō (1903–1975) is a masterful characterization, imbued with a profound Buddhist faith and at the same time a sensitive homage to his friend's artistic oeuvre. Munakata's torso, clad in a cotton kimono, rises into the picture like a mountain. The head turned slightly to a right in half-profile creates the compositional centre. The upper half is occupied by a near mirror image of a mandorla in which two Buddhist figures are seen, reaching almost beyond the margins of the block. Flame-shaped hatching fills the space on either side of the figure.

Sekino treats the gradation of tonalities with extreme skill. Body

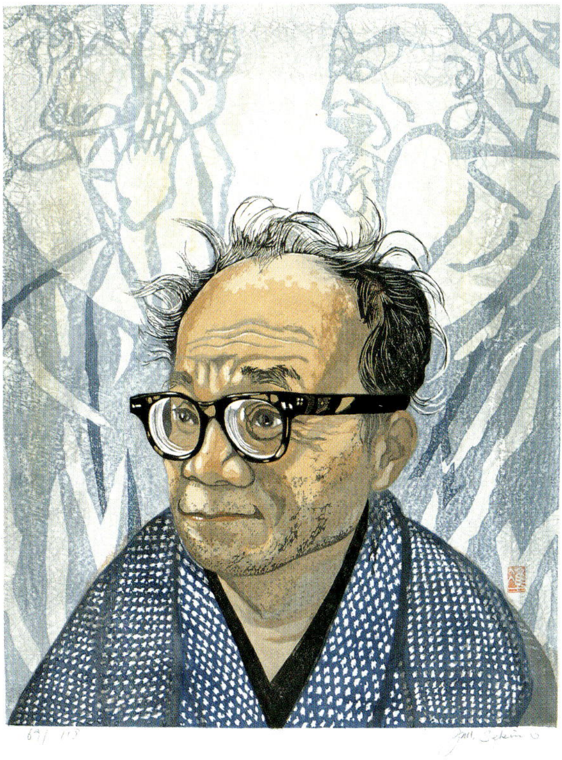

and features are marked by strong contour lines and shading. Moreover, the thick lenses of his glasses, deep furrows of his brow, and mussed hair of the old master are characterized by a radical realism, in marked contrast to the pictorial language of the background, which draws on the folk art, *mingei*, tradition.

Contextually and formally, Sekino quotes from one of the early masterpieces by Munakata Shikō. We can recognize Ubari, who compiled the Buddhist monastery rules, and Furuna, the leading preacher of Buddha's teachings, from Munakata's 1939 series "The Ten Great Disciples of the Buddha." In Sekino's portrait they are transformed into spiritual manifestations of the Buddha-like artist.

By emulating the form of traditional priest portraits (*juzō*) in the depiction of his teacher and friend, Sekino emphasizes the spiritual power of Munakata Shikō and his role as a model of the *sōsaku hanga* movement. It is perhaps also an allusion to the Buddhist honorific *hōgen* ("Eye of the Law"), which was bestowed on Munakata Shikō in January 1962.

Sekino created masterful drawings and woodcut portraits of Kabuki actors and Bunraku puppets before and during World War II, having seen the latter in performances at the Iwasaki factory in Tokyo. He is also renowned for his portraits of fellow artists such as Onchi Koshirō (1891–1955). For woodblock printing he tended to use *katsura* wood and handmade *tori-noko* paper, as did many of the *sōsaku hanga* artists. His later landscapes, such as the series "Fifty-three Stations of the Tōkaidō Road" begun in 1959 and completed in 1974, are remarkable for a calm and poetic visual language combined with brilliant technique. The masterful integration of the natural wood grain into the composition is typical of Sekino Jun'ichirō's work.

Strokes 81–10

Takeshi Hara (born 1942)
Lithograph, 83/100, circa 1980
Height 45 x 37.8 cm
Signed and marked on lower margin
Inv. No. 1999-16

Takeshi Hara was born in Nagoya and works and lives in Tokyo. All his graphic work is devoted to one motif, which he has repeated exclusively since the 1970s: strokes. The images present an astonishing variety, although they are all dominated by the same rhythmic movement of broad, zigzag brushstrokes from top to bottom.

With an extraordinary range of finely nuanced colours and additional accents – in this print, fine silver dust – Hara achieves a multitude of effects. The play between changing light and linear movement is Hara's main inspiration. In each instance he develops a very personal calligraphic formula with the utmost degree of objectivity. Hara's work is undoubtedly based on the calligraphic tradition of East Asia. The movements of brush and ink in the work of Takeshi Hara are not, however, the spontaneous ink application of traditional ink painting, but instead the decorative language and strident rhythm of pop art.

Hara thus combines his own cultural image tradition with Western attitudes. Takeshi Hara works mainly in etching, silkscreen printing, or, as in this example, a highly complex style of lithography. Since the late 1960s, all three printing techniques have become the favoured fine art printing techniques in Japan in addition to the traditional woodblock print. Artists such as Chimei Hamada (born 1917) and Gaku Onogi (1924–1976) were among the first to break with the at times overpowering influence of the *sosaku hanga kyokai* (Creative Print Association), founded at the beginning of the 20th century. They successfully countered the movement devoted exclusively to woodblock printing with experiments in European printing techniques. Takeshi's preference for lithography is founded in its ability to achieve brilliant colours and a gentle surface texture.

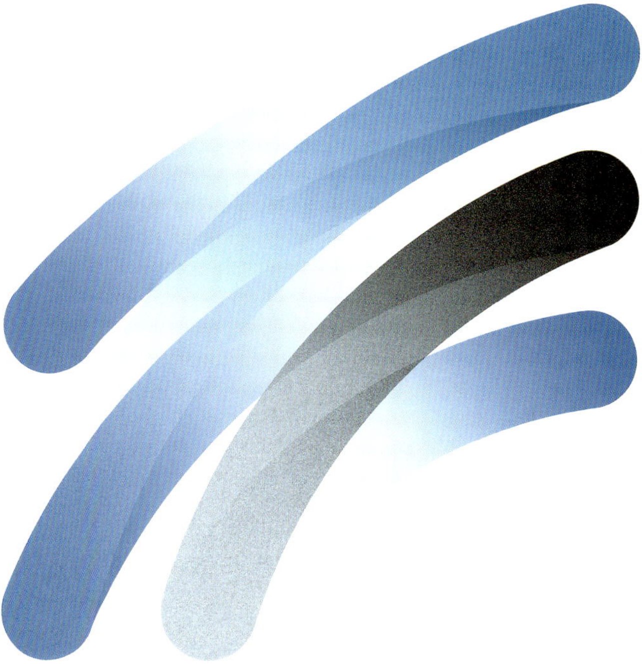

Chronological Table

China	Korea	Japan
	Neolithic Age to circa 800 BC	Jōmon period to circa 250 BC
Xia dynasty 21st–16th century BC Shang dynasty 16th–11th century BC Zhou dynasty 11th century–256 (221) BC		
	Bronze Age to circa 300 BC	
Qin dynasty 221–207 BC Han dynasty 206 BC–AD 220	Iron Age to circa 0	Yayoi period to circa AD 250
	Three Kingdoms period 57 BC–AD 668	
Three Kingdoms 220–265 (280) Northern and Southern Dynasties 265–581(589)		Kofun period 4th–7th century
Sui dynasty 589–618 Tang dynasty 618–906	Unified Silla period 668–935	Asuka period 552–644 Hakuhō period 645–710 Nara period 710–794 Heian period 794–1185
Five Dynasties 907–960 Liao dynasty 907–1125 Song dynasty 960–1279	Koryŏ period 935–1392	
Yuan dynasty 1279–1368		Kamakura period 1185–1333
Ming dynasty 1368–1644 Qing dynasty 1644–1911	Chosŏn period 1392–1910	Muromachi period 1333–1573 Momoyama period 1573–1614 Edo period (Tokugawa) (1603) 1614–1868 Meiji period 1868-1912
Republic 1912–	Japanese Rule 1910–1945	Taishō period 1912–1926 Shōwa period 1926–1989
People's Republic 1949–	North and South Korea 1945–	Heisei period 1989–